# Housing Boom and Bust

Housing markets depend on long-term borrowing. This borrowing comes from banks and mortgage lenders who are players in international financial markets. They borrow and lend across borders and often use mortgage debt as a form of security for their borrowing. In other words, they use debt to create more debt.

It has been taken for granted that housing was a good investment and would provide wealth and security for the current generation and the next. Yet housing is prone to speculative bubbles with rapid house price inflation and is subject to 'irrational exuberance', where people begin to believe that they can only gain from investing in property. But, as we are now seeing, these bubbles eventually burst and create economic misery for millions. Moreover, it appears that policy makers, bankers and households never learn that a bust always follows a boom. Yet the culture of property ownership has become so ingrained over the last 30 years that it is difficult for any government to do anything but support the tenure. Governments in the US, Europe and the UK have consistently supported it financially and rhetorically to the extent that owner occupation is now seen as the normal expectation.

Peter King looks at how the current crisis in housing markets has arisen. He considers the causes of house price bubbles and the reasons for the collapse in markets worldwide – are these problems integral to markets or could they have been avoided? Is government regulation the solution or part of the cause? This book explains the ways in which future booms and busts can be mitigated and how the lessons of this latest housing bubble can – finally – be learnt.

**Peter King** is Reader in Social Thought in the Centre for Comparative Housing Research at De Montfort University, Leicester. The second edition of his book *Understanding Housing Finance* was published by Routledge in 2009.

# Housing Boom and Bust

Owner occupation, government regulation and the credit crunch

Peter King

Routledge
Taylor & Francis Group

LONDON AND NEW YORK

First published 2010
by Routledge
2 Park Square, Milton Park, Abingdon, Oxon, OX14 4RN

Simultaneously published in the USA and Canada
by Routledge
270 Madison Avenue, New York, NY 10016

*Routledge is an imprint of the Taylor & Francis Group,
an informa business*

© 2010 Peter King

Typeset in Sabon by
Florence Production Ltd, Stoodleigh, Devon
Printed and bound in Great Britain by
TJ International Ltd, Padstow, Cornwall

*British Library Cataloguing in Publication Data*
A catalogue record for this book is available from the British Library

*Library of Congress Cataloging-in-Publication Data*
King, Peter, 1960–
Housing boom and bust : owner occupation, government regulation
and the credit crunch / Peter King.
    p. cm.
Includes bibliographical references and index.
1. Housing. 2. Home ownership. 3. Housing policy. 4. Housing—
Finance. I. Title.
HD7287.K5584 2010
333.33'8—dc22                                          2009027236

ISBN10: 0–415–55313–X (hbk)
ISBN10: 0–415–55314–8 (pbk)
ISBN10: 0–203–86176–0 (ebk)

ISBN13: 978–0–415–55313–1 (hbk)
ISBN13: 978–0–415–55314–8 (pbk)
ISBN13: 978–0–203–86176–9 (ebk)

To B, H and R,
as always

# Contents

# Preface

One evening in late 2008 my daughter Helen was sitting reading in the armchair by the window. She was disturbed when I came in muttering about some bad news – more redundancies or retailers going bust, or possibly both. 'This is looking really bad!' I said. Helen looked up from her book, startled for a moment. 'But, we're OK, aren't we?' she asked. 'Well, yes, I suppose we are,' I said, a bit nonplussed. 'Then it's all right, isn't it?' she said, and went back to her book, ignoring my mouth flapping open and shut noiselessly.

My first thought was to see her response as perhaps just a little offhand, callous even. You might put it down to being a teenager and all that. But Helen is not really the 'Yeah, whatever' type: she is an intelligent and enquiring young person who, despite claiming to have no interest in her father's rants, studies politics at an after-school class and knows more than she lets on. So perhaps, I thought, what if she was actually saying something important? That us being all right was what actually mattered. The result of that thought is this book, written as it is in all its apparent perversity and self-knowing. This book, I might claim, is a view of the credit crunch from the armchair by the window.

What Helen had hit on was the manner in which most of us, most of the time, relate to a crisis. Our first reaction is to show concern, anxiety even. We have a quick and urgent need to be reassured, to be told that everything is all right, and then we can settle down again. This does not mean that we do not care about others or that we are being in any way callous. Rather it shows that our concern has limits and that it tends to be focused on what is there in front of us. Helen's reaction showed how we tend to filter events and assimilate them into our own little world. Helen, like everyone, gets exercised about certain things – climate change, animal cruelty, the stupidity of men, unnecessary wars, and so on – but she also has a life to lead and interests to pursue, friends to meet and exams to pass. Like most of us, she tends to hold onto those things closest to her. And it wasn't the daily news items about the credit crunch that bothered her – they were too general – but the fact that her uncle lost his job in late 2008. Like most of us, she has to pick and choose what she gets bothered about.

My reason for discussing this little incident is not to embarrass my daughter (not that she will believe me), but to suggest that this is actually how we do tend to view the world. There is us in here, and then there are others out there. We know what is going on out there, but there remains a distance, a separation between us and the world outside. We distinguish quite naturally between the personal and the general, between things that happen and things that happen to us. We concentrate inevitably on what touches us, as opposed to what is just going on, even though the latter might seem more important.

This is a book that starts from the inside and looks out. I wanted to understand the financial crisis not just as a worldwide all-encompassing event – which it certainly appears to be – but also from the perspective of individual households, with their mortgages, their bills and debts, as well as the thousand and one petty concerns that cross before them on an average day. I wanted to look at how we use markets, not in a textbook sense, or even from a particular economic perspective, but as individuals who relate to objects based on our needs, desires and aspirations. Just what is it that we expect from markets and so how do we present ourselves to them?

One of my concerns in doing this was a worry that some were using the financial crisis – caused, in part at least, by a collapse in housing markets – as an excuse to question the manner in which most households in the UK and US relate to their housing. In February 2009, I took part in a debate on the housing opportunities for young people, hosted by BBC Radio Leicester. The young people there were very aware of the issues of affordability and shortage and, quite naturally, wanted answers from the assembled experts. Many of the young people prefaced their questions with phrases such as 'When I buy ...' or 'How can I buy ... ?', and I must admit I didn't particularly notice this until it was pointed out by one of the panel. From that moment on, however, the discussion was turned into a series of declarations on the virtues of social renting and the evils of owner occupation. The audience of young people was told in no uncertain terms that they should not expect to buy their own home, but that rather they should live in social housing. They should be demanding that the government builds more rented housing rather than merely thinking about how they can afford to buy.

What struck me was the almost complete disjuncture between the aspirations of young people to own – even in a recession – and the attitude of housing professionals who saw their role as that of promoting social renting. Indeed, there was a sense of triumphalism from some of the adults in the audience that housing markets were in a state of collapse, and that finally people might stop 'deluding' themselves that owning was a better option that social renting.

Interestingly, a show of hands at the end of the discussion showed that most of the audience was not convinced about the evils of ownership. However, Britain in 2009 is not a particularly receptive place in which to extol the virtue of housing markets. Indeed some might actually argue that this is the perfect time to rethink our attitudes to housing and owner occupation in particular. They might argue that the fetishisation of property ownership has proven disastrous and so we should focus now on other tenures, and concentrate on need rather than aspiration.

But what if these young people in Leicester were also right, and that instead of telling them they are deluded, we actually listened when they say, 'When I buy ...', and respect them for it? Might we not then start to understand how people, here and now, actually do relate to housing, rather than just assuming that we – the grown-ups – know better?

In this book I assume that these young people are indeed right, and argue accordingly. The discussions, speculations and arguments in this book spring from the assumption that we wish to protect those things close to us and that what matters about our housing – what makes it meaningful – is how we use it. This gives me a perspective on the collapse of housing markets, which I believe is both distinctive and important.

What is particular about the housing boom and bust of the first decade of the twenty-first century is that, in the Anglosphere and beyond, it is the first time that there is no practical alternative to owner occupation. Private renting is seen by many as a temporary staging post, and social housing has declined in the UK over the last 30 years so that it now consists of less than 20 per cent of households. In addition, it suffers from what we might call an image problem and is not considered by many as a suitable long-term option. In contrast, just over 70 per cent of UK households are owner occupiers, and this means that, regardless of what its critics might say, there simply is no viable alternative to it. So this is perhaps the first recession when the only alternative to a housing market that does not work is one that does.

This dominance of owner occupation means, however, that we have both a clear set of expectations to work towards – we know what a successful resolution means – but it also suggests that we have less room to manoeuvre. We cannot put forward any practical alternatives to what is currently there. We can, of course, tinker with aspects of the banking system and make changes to how mortgage lenders are regulated and overseen, but what we cannot do is shift to a different set of structures. We might not even be able to rebalance matters very much: both main forms of renting suffer in comparison to owning, and there seems little to suggest that this imbalance can be altered. Mostly this is because not enough people want to rent, and in a democracy that has to be respected. The majority of households are not calling for an alternative to owner occupation, but rather a more stable version of what we now have.

This is the situation that we have to start with, and it has deeply influenced the manner in which I have approached this discussion on housing boom and bust. Unless we properly appreciate how we use our housing and what it means to us, we will be unable to come up with any suitable remedies.

Taking the view from the armchair by the window also suggests another key aspect of housing. Much of the discussion about housing is based on standards and aggregates, and this is a position I have argued against for many years (King 1996, 2003, 2008). The financial crisis, however, seems to have emphasised this trend. All the discussion is about numbers and they tend to be getting larger. We no longer get impressed when central bankers and politicians talk about billions: it has to be at least a trillion for anyone to notice. Likewise, the focus of the housing debate is the percentage fall in house prices, the number of repossessions/foreclosures, the number of sales, how much they are down on the previous years, and so on.

What is missing is the private and personal nature of this crisis. Instead of looking at numbers, we should focus on personal tragedies caused by unemployment, unmanageable debt and the loss of one's home. What we should be focusing on is the fact that in some households there are parents who are unable to tell their children that it is all right. Our housing surrounds our most private activities, and simply referring to where we live as an investment or as an asset seriously diminishes its meaning for us.

But these tragedies have come about because of particular actions that individuals have taken, some of which might have been unlucky, whilst others were ill-advised. The other side of the personal, therefore, is responsibility, and we need to question just how far individual households are implicated in the crisis. One effect of seeing owner occupation as a delusion – as dependent for its success on 'hegemonic discourses' – is to exonerate any individual of responsibility for their own actions. If we are being duped by dominant interests in society to believe that owner occupation is the best option, then we cannot be held to account once this house of cards collapses.

However, if we accept it is reasonable to have the desire to own, then we also have to suggest that we should bear the consequences of our actions; that, to a considerable extent, it is for us to make sure that we are all right and should not seek to blame others or to seek undue redress. Of course not all problems are our fault, and we are simply not capable of dealing personally with economic problems on the scale we are facing in 2009. But this does not mean that we can expect to be bailed out or that we will not be affected in some permanent and significant way. The financial wave hits us indiscriminately, without favour, so what matters is how prepared we are to deal with it. Have we taken the necessary precautions and built in some margin of safety, or have we just trusted to luck and hoped that we will be all right?

As a result of asking these questions, and seeing housing boom and bust in personal terms, I reach a number of conclusions about how we might deal with future problems. Perhaps unsurprisingly, my conclusions do not depend particularly on new forms of financial engineering, but rather relate to our attitudes towards housing. What we need is not, or not just, better banks and more sensible government regulation, but a different way of looking at our housing that depends less on finance and collateral and more on its existential significance as a place of safety, comfort and (physical and emotional) security.

A final point: it quickly became apparent when I started work on this book that it was an incredibly stupid thing to have undertaken. There have been many attempts to create a link between the crisis of 2008 with the Great Depression of the 1930s. However, what struck me about this earlier period was not so much the similarities and differences, but the fact that historians and economists still cannot agree on what really caused it and which actions solved it. But if we cannot decide on these matters 80 years later, what chance do I have of coming to any sensible conclusions before this crisis is actually over? What makes it worse is that the nature of the crisis appears to change week by week, with different emphases and prospects appearing and disappearing with almost unbelievable speed. World stock markets go up and down and no one seems to know quite why. In March 2009 one set of data reported an increase in UK house prices, but this was promptly contradicted by data that came out only a few days later. Some commentators claim to see the green shoots of recovery, whilst others only see it getting much worse.

What this suggests, of course, is that no one really knows. The problem of committing oneself to print, therefore, is that one can look pretty silly if the wind changes and things suddenly start to look different. This, though, is but another reason to take the particular tack I have in this book, with the rather long exposition in Chapter 2 of how we can relate our use of housing to markets. My aim was not to undertake instant commentary – that is for journalists, who are much faster on their feet than I am – but to assess housing boom and bust in a more holistic context. I hope, therefore, that this book will remain of some use even after the current crisis is over.

I have a number of people to thank for their help in the course of this project. Alex Hollingsworth and Catherine Lynn at Routledge have been very supportive throughout this project. I should also thank the anonymous reviewers who made numerous suggestions to improve the scope and content of the book. My sister-in-law Sheila has again taken on the gargantuan task of correcting my grammar and if this text is anywhere near readable it is entirely down to her.

My colleagues at the Centre for Comparative Housing Research remain a constant source of support, wisdom and inspiration. Jo Richardson has read and commented on parts of the book, as well as listening and responding to many of my ideas on journeys to and from Leicester. I have also benefited from the comments of both Tim Brown and Mike Oxley, particularly on the material in Chapter 2. Those students who took my module 'Housing Markets and the State' in 2008–9 also deserve special mention, both for putting up with my enthusiasms and for responding in kind. A fair bit of what follows has been sparked by their challenging questions and comments.

As I have made clear, I owe a lot to my family, particularly the sceptical eyebrows of my eldest daughter, Helen. Her sister, Rachel, has always been prepared to ask about my projects and seems interested in what I tell her. She did tell me, however, the very worst joke. What is a banker's favourite breakfast cereal? Credit crunch! Oh, how we laughed. My wife, B, puts up with a lot because of my intense ways of working and my anxieties and obsessions. Yet she is also the one who can put it all in perspective, and she can do this simply by being here.

Peter King
June 2009

# Chapter 1

# Housing is not finance

Housing, we now find, is something that is both very local, yet also very global. It is close to us, literally surrounding us, providing our personal space. But it also connects us to what is distant, unfamiliar and impersonal. Housing locates us in a particular place and keeps us secure and comfortable. Yet we now see that the ways in which we gain access to it, maintain it and pay for it link us into global financial markets.

Housing markets depend on long-term borrowing. This borrowing comes from banks and mortgage lenders who are players in international financial markets. They borrow and lend across borders and often use our mortgage debt as a form of security for their borrowing. In other words, they use our debt to create more debt. And so the housing decisions we take in Detroit, Los Angeles, Derby or Lincoln link us to Frankfurt, Tokyo, Wall Street and the City of London. Many people, it now appears, have a stake in our little homestead.

It has been a taken-for-granted assumption for several decades now, in both the UK and the US, that housing is a good investment that will provide wealth and security for the current generation and the next (Ferguson 2008). Yet housing, from time to time, is prone to speculative bubbles, which see rapid house price inflation with the consequent rush to buy a house before it becomes completely unaffordable. The market is subject to what former Federal Reserve chairperson Alan Greenspan famously referred to as 'irrational exuberance', when people begin to believe that they can only gain from investing in property

(Shiller 2005, 2008). But, as we have been reminded again, these bubbles eventually burst, and the debt used to create more debt has turned out to be toxic.

Our housing – where we live, what we call my home – is not about boom and bust. We think that it exists to be regular, to provide us with a stable platform for our lives. Our dwelling is the background in front of which we play out our lives (King 2005). Our housing, we hope, is the very opposite of a toxic asset. It is a place of safety and security (King 2004): the benign means to achieve our ends.

Boom and bust, we like to think, is what takes place outside the house, somewhere beyond our boundary. It exists outside our own little world where we feel in control. We do not want it to encroach and we can use our dwelling to help achieve this. We regard it as a fortress, a structure that is impermeable. It is resistant to ingress, and we are comforted by this. We can hide here, feel secure, we can be ourselves here. We can cut ourselves off, be with those – and only those – we wish. We are protected from the world in here.

We tend to separate out our daily lives from any sense of crisis. The financial crisis is an external entity. We get to know about it through the media, and get angry about the excesses of bankers and the incompetence and self-serving of politicians. We fulminate about the apparent greed of bankers who demand bail-outs but keep their bonuses. We despair at politicians who argue that they could not possibly be blamed for the crisis, but insist they are the only ones who can sort it out.

But for most of us, most of the time, the crisis does not impact upon us directly. Of course, as the crisis continues, we are more likely to know some of those who are affected – friends or family members who have lost their jobs or are in danger of repossession or foreclosure – and are more likely to be affected ourselves. But those affected are still in the minority. For most of us, the crisis is still somehow separate from us and distinct from how we act, behave and seek to live. We carry on with the same activities, doing the same things and will do so unless and until something happens. We carry on until we ourselves are hit. And then it is all terribly serious. We now face a huge personal crisis, which we might be unable to cope with and which we could not prepare for.

I have deliberately here emphasised the word 'personal' because this, it seems to me, is entirely the point. There is a necessary distinction to be made between the personal and the general. By this I mean we should distinguish between what is happening in general – namely, a crisis that is out there – with what is now, at this very moment in all its palpable certainty, happening to us. We can feel sorry for, and empathise with, those losing their jobs and dwellings, and we might think that, but for the grace of God, it could be us, but there remains a distance that separates the hypothetical from the concrete. This has nothing to do with callousness or ignorance of the needs of others (King 2004), but is rather our imperative to concentrate on ourselves and our own, with those closest and dearest to us. The enclosing aspect of dwelling (King 2008) helps us to do this. We can insulate ourselves so we can protect those we love, as well as ourselves.

This capability to use a dwelling to enclose ourselves makes the impact of any loss all the greater for us. This is because of our ability to take how we live and our housing for granted. What we have is an object which we are so absorbed in that we tend not to notice it, but whose loss would be absolutely catastrophic for us. It hits us personally, particularly and peculiarly, such that any generalities about the nature of the financial crisis become irrelevant.

Housing, we might think, is not the same as finance. Housing is something different. Housing is physical objects, places of refuge, comfort and security (King 2004). Yet we can attach ourselves to these objects only if we have the means. We need finance to allow us to gain access to housing (King 2009). But housing, we tend to think, provides us with a place to live.

But increasingly it appears that finance has become the end of housing. Our housing is an investment, an asset and a store of wealth: it is property. Of course it has always been these things, in potential at least. But we might say that the finance has started to subsume the dwelling, so that now we take it first and foremost as an asset – as an object we use as collateral. It becomes not a means for the fulfilment of needs, but a means for progression, for financial growth and development. Our housing, we think, will make us wealthy.

The danger of this position is that we stop being satisfied with our dwelling for what it is, but rather for what it can become. We divorce – a peculiarly appropriate word here – the use we make of the dwelling from the meaning we attach to it. We still use the dwelling but we attribute a financial rather than an existential meaning to it. The dwelling becomes potential. This is what an investment is: a becoming, a development, a movement from here to there. The dwelling is now seen increasingly as a place of potential, of a step towards another place or another state. Our current place is only a staging post, a place to rest and recoup as we plot the next stage of our journey upwards (King 2004).

It is quite appropriate that we use the image of climbing the property ladder. We seek to get on the ladder and, once we are on, we are safe, we have 'made it'. We now feel we can climb the ladder, trading up to find our perfect dwelling. But the main thing is that we are actually on the ladder.

However, I must say, as someone who once found himself at the top of one when my dear brother decided to move it, I have always been somewhat dubious about ladders. I like to know just what a ladder is resting on and that it is leaning securely against something. I want to know that it is actually securely held and stable and not in danger of toppling. I also want to know if I can trust the person holding it steady. And, being of a cautious cast of mind, I need to know where the ladder actually leads, other than just up. Is it possible to actually get to the top and, if we could, what would we do when we got there? Would we just sit there, or simply come back down again? Is there any point to climbing it in the first place?

A ladder is a tool: normally we use it to help us reach something, or to get somewhere. We use it to move ourselves to a higher level, so we can reach further than we otherwise would. But this does not seem to be the case with the property ladder. Its destination is always left unmentioned. It has no end as far we can see, but merely one rung after another. What we seek to do, or are told we need to do, is to get on the ladder and then to remain on it. We might seek to go upwards, but what for? Where are we going and would we even know if we got there? Being on the property ladder becomes an end in itself, a proverbial 'good thing'.

What concerns me about ladders is that if they slip and fall, as they invariably seem to do, then so do we. Falling off a ladder can cause us a lot of damage, but the property ladder is not like a real ladder in this regard. I don't mean that we won't get hurt, indeed quite the reverse. Unlike a real ladder, we can hurt ourselves just as much by falling from the bottom rung of the property ladder as from the top. Being on the lowest rung is no guarantee against disaster. The property ladder is an 'all or nothing' experience and our commitment has to be total. This means that the effect of a fall, from whichever rung, can be just as damaging.

We can now see that the metaphor of the ladder works only one way. We only go up the ladder. We seldom consider a downward journey, and this is because it can be quite difficult for us to come down safely. Instead of a ladder perhaps we should use the image of the escalator, which is set to go only one way. This might make the journey easier: we are assisted by the escalator itself and everyone is going in the same direction. But it is only useful if that is the direction we want to take. It is hard to stop it, and it is very difficult to change direction and go against the flow.

Also the image of the escalator is an improvement on the ladder because it suggests moving, trading up to ever better properties, using the equity in one to help fund the next. But it is this very idea of moving upwards that is problematic. If we use our dwelling as an asset, as something we seek to build on, and if we see ourselves as having a 'housing career', in which we move from one dwelling to another and so maximise our financial situation, we are, in truth, taking a risk with our dwelling. This risk is that we are using our dwelling – our home – as a means to achieve a non-housing end. We are using it for a purpose other than dwelling.

As Niall Ferguson (2008) has stated, the risk in a situation like this is that we transfer our security to others. We think our house is safe, but it is safe only if we have the means to continue funding it. The security is our income, and the property is somebody else's security. If we lose our income, others are protected, but we are not. If we die, we can leave the asset to our children, and so it can be seen as security for them, and this doubtless provides us with some comfort. Yet it is again literally at our expense, and the dwelling is still just an asset. Our children may have seen this dwelling at one time as the family home, but on the death of their parents, when it is emptied of people and things and the relations between them, it is reduced merely to an asset: a thing with a monetary value and a means to greater security. This is not, we hope, because they are callous or glad to see us gone, but because they are likely to be well-housed already.

Is not the real security, on a day-to-day practical level, gained from the physicality of the dwelling and the relations it supports, rather than its quality as an asset? It is the fact that our dwelling keeps us warm, dry, safe and secure that matters. It is that the dwelling acts as a store of memories and as a place of intimacy that we really need (King 2004). Or perhaps stated more practically, we can only find financial security in our dwelling once we are secure in the physicality of the dwelling. Of course we need the income to gain the dwelling and continue to stay there, but this is a concern for the moment and not for the future. We live in a manner based on short-term regularities, of day-in-day-out activities within a particular dwelling in its specific environment. We dwell in and on the possible, on what the dwelling actually does and is. We open ourselves up to risk when we see the dwelling as potential, as a not-quite-yet emerging possibility, or of something that is just over the horizon, but never actually in clear sight. Our dwelling, properly speaking, is never a work in progress, but always finished as it is, as an object in use. We can dwell only in this moment. This does not mean we should forget the future or aspire to something else. But we should not use what is here now merely for what might be elsewhere.

Of course owner occupiers do not usually consider that they are taking a risk when buying a house by taking out a mortgage. They are doing something safe and expected – as safe as houses, as the cliché goes. This is just what we do and what everyone else is doing. It is normal, taken for granted, and certainly not risky. It is, as far as we are concerned, about getting on with the way we live now. This might be a misperception, and in hindsight many people might be judged to have acted foolishly, but is there any rational reason to have expected them to have behaved differently at the time? Despite previous house price crashes, people clearly do not expect the housing market to fall – they cannot foresee themselves falling off the ladder – and so they do not see buying houses as being particularly risky.

But this very sense of safety, of living apparently free from risk, allows us to aspire and to think of what might be if only we had a bigger house, or moved to a different part of town. We can aspire because, all the time, we sense we are safe where we are. Our dwelling can be the platform for our desires and our dreams, and it can give us the basis upon which to plan for our ascent. Here we begin to see something of a paradox, which, I want to suggest, is of crucial importance to any debate about boom and bust in housing markets. We see our housing as safe, and so we speculate. Our housing gives us a sense that we can aspire, but what we are speculating on is our housing, the very basis of our need for safety and security.

So we can certainly state that housing is not the same as finance. We need to differentiate between the existential and the economic (King 1996; Turner 1976) and not confuse means with ends. The trouble is that our housing can work so well for us that we lose sight of how we use it, and we seek to do more, to extend ourselves and stretch for a higher rung.

There is a danger that the crisis might be used to attack certain institutions. Some will use the collapse of housing markets to criticise capitalism in general, particularly the Anglo-Saxon version of it. They will argue that they were right in being sceptical of the Thatcher/Reagan legacy all along, and that as this period is now so clearly over we can return to a period of more active government. More prosaically, some will use the crisis to criticise owner occupation and argue that there is something inherently unstable about the tenure, with crashes coming with some regularity every ten to 15 years. Those who suggest that owner occupation is merely an ideological construction or hegemonic discourse used to disguise a particular interest (Jacobs *et al.* 2003; Kemeny 1981, 2005; Ronald 2008) can point to the crisis and suggest that reform is necessary. What is needed, so the argument runs, is to rebalance housing tenures to ensure that owner occupation is only one tenure among several and not the dominant one. In the UK this has led to calls for the building of more social housing or to develop shared-ownership products that offer some shielding from the vicissitudes of the market. More generally, there are calls for greater government regulation of markets to ensure that this type of boom and bust does not happen again. This position, of course, is as ideological as the so-called 'hegemonic discourses' it seeks to challenge. It is based on a series of assumptions about housing as an entirely public or social entity, in which the dominant concern is to meet aggregated need rather than having anything to do with aspiration and the existential significance of housing as a store of meaning, as well as a place of physical safety and security.

This does not help us to understand why so many people want to become owner occupiers. Why has it become so dominant, particularly in the Anglo-Saxon countries, but also in European countries like Spain? As we have seen, critics, like Jacobs *et al.* (2003) and Kemeny (1981), assume that this is irrational or is a constructed discourse built by government policies and rhetoric, and therefore a change in that policy and rhetoric could alter the situation. These critics tend to look to other countries, particularly in Europe, where owner occupation is less dominant to demonstrate that there is nothing natural with regard to owning. Owner occupation is lower in Germany which, like France, has not had the speculative house price increases of the US or UK. Therefore it is assumed that the problem is specific to a form of Anglo-American capitalism.

First, we should note that this tends to be a rather selective argument, in that critics of owner occupation tend to ignore a number of eurozone countries, such as Ireland and Spain, which have experienced similar housing booms and the consequent collapse. But, second, we can question the very technique of social constructionism as applied to this debate. In particular, why should we assume that the particular legal, cultural and institutional arrangements in Germany are not as socially constructed, and therefore as contingent as those in the UK and US? Why should it be owner occupation that is the ideological construct and not particular forms of renting? On what basis should we treat the German or French situation as being more 'normal' or 'natural'? Social constructionists might argue that neither is natural and all tenure relations are constructions. If this is the case, then the argument is reduced to a banality and has little intellectual substance. Of course they might indeed be correct that no form of tenure is in any way 'natural'. But what we might argue instead – and this is consistent with the constructionist position – is that in Anglo-Saxon countries the incentives and conditions are right for owning to prosper, and if these conditions pertained elsewhere then so might high levels of property ownership. This can be only speculation, but it is of the same status as that of critics of owner occupation who call for a rebalancing in favour of renting.

What is important is that we do not lose sight of what owner occupation and housing markets actually have and do achieve. It is, of course, harder in certain times than others to suggest that markets do work well and are the most efficient form of allocating scarce resources. But, by the same token, we should not throw out the many benefits of markets because they do not operate to their optimum. Even in the depth of a recession, we need to remember that most households are not in mortgage arrears or negative equity or at risk of losing their dwelling. As Akerlof and Shiller (2009) have pointed out, there is a natural tendency to place economic data in a negative light. Hence, they state, the figure of 25 per cent unemployment during the Great Depression is always given and not the fact that 75 per cent of American workers stayed in work. They suggest that there are good reasons for stressing the one figure rather than the other – we wish to deal with problems, not ignore them – but also that, even in this most traumatic of economic crises, capitalism was still working after a fashion.

In making this point, it is not my aim to minimise the personal tragedy of those affected. Indeed, as I have stated above, my aim is to stress the personal nature of the tragedy and not to reduce it to one statistic amongst many. It matters precisely because it is personal, affecting the dreams, aspirations and well-being of specific individuals. But still, for most individuals, these aspirations remain intact, even if we might be aware that we are less well placed than we might have been a year or so earlier.

Much of the discussion around the financial crisis is conducted in absolute terms. The Anglo-Saxon model of capitalism is described as fundamentalist and based on an extreme form of laissez-faire. Yet the governments of the US and UK are not the minimalist states called for by libertarian thinkers such as Nozick (1974). Indeed both these governments have extended their reach over the last decade in terms of spending and intrusive legislation restricting individual liberties. The US and UK might be more liberal in economic terms than many European countries but they are hardly bastions of anarcho-capitalism. Likewise, economic activity in Europe and Asia is based on markets open to international trade and competition. The differences are therefore of degree rather than absolute principle, and this needs to be remembered when discussing any reforms to housing or the economy more generally.

Might this mean, then, that the financial crisis of 2008 is not really about owner occupation at all? We can, and should, make a practical distinction between how we use our dwelling and housing markets, which is where we buy and sell dwellings. The state of housing markets matters to me professionally as an academic, but, if I am honest, it does not matter to me as an owner occupier. I do not personally need to move; I can afford where I live and like my current dwelling. I have no real reason to change, and so don't see why I should. I would suggest that most households are in a similar position. Most people, most of the time, are settled and so do not need to relate to housing markets. We are looking inwards to our dwelling and its contents and not outwards into the market. We may be aware that the value of our dwelling has declined somewhat, but do not see this as a problem we need to face.

The problems at present are with housing and financial markets, but not with owner occupation, where owner occupation is taken as just a particular means of sustaining access to housing. We can use our dwellings just as well as we did before the crisis started in 2008, and, for most of us, our situations are eminently sustainable. There is a clear need to sort out the problems with particular markets and institutions and try to ensure that this does not recur. But these are matters of regulation and financial engineering: they are the concern for matters like system design and management capability, but not our specific relation to housing as such.

Instead of criticising owner occupation and calling for its replacement, we should be focusing on the relationship that individual households have with markets when they need to enter them. What I mean by this is not the abstractions of micro-economic theory, as useful as they can be, but rather the manner in which personal aims and aspirations motivate us to move into and out of markets. Once we appreciate how individuals relate to markets, we can then gain a fuller picture of the crisis and properly locate its meaning. This is in the belief that the proper focus of housing – why it is significant – is as a private activity. Accordingly, the essence of any discussion should be to retain what housing means to individuals and not to seek remedies that are inconsistent with this.

The aim of this book, therefore, is to consider housing boom and bust from the perspective of the desire to own. This entails an understanding of the subjective relations and attitudes to markets at the household level before we can properly undertake to consider the role of government regulation and the nature of the crisis. My aim is to distinguish quite purposefully between the individual level of decision-making, what I choose to call really private finance, and the corporate decision-making linked to government policy and practice.

Governments, in the UK, US and elsewhere, over the last 30 years have sought to liberalise markets and to encourage private action. However, they have done this not through withdrawing their reach, but rather through active regulation and involvement. The result has been a rather skewed development of markets which have favoured large corporations and interests at the expense of consumers and small producers. Indeed much of the brunt of regulation has focused on the micro level and ignored the action of larger interests. The result, from the point of view of housing in the UK, has been increasing regulation at the level of house selling and the local planning system, but with a reduction in oversight of national and international financial institutions.

The key narrative to this book is that the current problems in housing markets are not with owner occupation as such, but rather with how government misunderstands markets and regulates badly, and how financial institutions have been able to take advantage of this naivety. Any remedies to the crisis have to be seen on the basis of households' relations to housing markets and not the interests of financial institutions. These remedies should therefore be realistic and proportionate and not turn the crisis into a critique of owner occupation. We need to distinguish clearly between the use we can, and do, make of our housing and market relations. This is not to denigrate the role of markets, which are generally the most effective and efficient means of allocating resources. But rather it is an attempt to prevent the opportunistic denigration of markets from tainting the particular relations we have with our housing.

Opportunism tends to succeed when it is able to produce a simple story in which a straightforward chain of causality can be shown. Such a story should leave no one in doubt as to who is to blame. But the reality of a situation is never so simple. Imagine a child's balloon in the shape of the archetypal house: a square shape with a door and three windows, sloping roof and a chimney. As it gets near to its full size, the child can see how attractive a design it is, and she is excited as the shape begins to form. The child wants the pretty shape, she finds it beguiling. But she is not exactly sure when to stop blowing it up and she might get carried away. If she keeps blowing in air, we know what will happen – the balloon will get bigger still and the shape of the house will start to deform. It will stretch and distend and its colour will seem to drain as the plastic gets thinner and thinner. Eventually it will burst. But the child does not know exactly when this will happen; she might think that one more breath won't make any difference and so she goes on. She can only know it was a silly thing to do with hindsight, when it was too late. Only then does she regret the last breath, of taking that extra risk and going just that tiny bit further. But, she moans, it was only a tiny little bit extra, no bigger than any that preceded it. Yet the last breath was only significant because of all those that preceded it. It was the accumulation of those breaths that made the last one so consequential. So we might say that it wasn't the last act that mattered but the aggregate of actions. It was all part of a development, a progression. We can see what caused the balloon to burst as a series of tiny progressions, all of them optimistic, hopeful, until, finally, disaster strikes. We naturally blame the last action, the one that 'caused' the balloon to burst. But it was not just this last one that had the effect but the combined impact of all of them.

There is an important lesson in this trite little story of the child's balloon, and it is an all-too-obvious one. We might focus on individual incidents that seem to have precipitated a crisis. One in particular seems to be the cause. The link is apparently clear: that last breath and then 'bang'. But it was just one act that followed many other similar ones. None of these acts was of itself consequential. Instead they have to be taken together with others: the problem with the balloon was the volume of air, not that final breath. It is when many incidents and acts come together in a certain manner that we are at risk and leave ourselves vulnerable. As a whole, these little actions, each one insignificant in itself, can be disastrous. But it is only in the end, and at the point where they cannot be separated, that this risk becomes clear to us. In the end there is just a general volume, and it doesn't matter then which breath caused the explosion. The outcome is the same.

Most of us, even young children, know that if we blow up a balloon too far, it will burst. We know that the more we put in, the riskier it gets, even if we cannot precisely say when we should stop. What this suggests is that whilst we need to be aware of accumulated consequences, of how one action builds on, and links to, another, we also need to be aware that not all actions carry an equal risk, and some actions matter more than others precisely because of what precedes them. The problem, though, is that each action is much like another. They are all similar and appear equally useful and purposeful. So why should one matter more than any other? We need to be most careful precisely when we feel we are benefiting from these actions, when we are enjoying the effect of the balloon taking shape, getting bigger and bigger and think it is down to our own efforts. We can then lose sight of our goal and go too far, egged on by our own enthusiasm.

This book, then, can be seen as an exercise in gentle deflation, of trying to bring things down without a big bang. My approach is not to consider new ways of regulating housing or altering the planning system, nor do I seek to plan out a new financial architecture for the global economy. My aims are both much more minimalist and more far reaching than this. What I rather do is question the manner in which we view housing. I look at what makes housing significant and I conclude that it is not finance. Housing is meaningful because of how we are able to use it. We need money to allow us to do this, but this is just a means, and what really matters is what we have used it on and for. My aim, therefore, is to try to change the attitudes we have towards housing: to show that it is private and not public, and that it is about stability rather than change. This means we need to question our understanding of housing and how it links into markets. We need to be clear about what housing is for, and, most of all, to be aware that housing and finance are not one and the same.

# Chapter 2

# Really private finance

## Introduction

I live in blissful ignorance of the value of my house. I know how much we paid for it in 1993 and I know how much I have to pay each month on my mortgage and I also, having just looked it up, know when we make the last payment to the bank and so when the dwelling will actually be ours. I could probably make a very rough guess at the house's current value and I could certainly find some reasonably precise information on one of the various websites that exist to help us buy and sell property. However, I have never seen the need to bother. What matters more to me is whether we can afford to live here – which we can comfortably – and whether the house still fits our needs – which I suppose it does, as long as I don't ask my teenage daughters if they have enough space.

I know that the value of my house has fallen and that, if it is typical of the average, it will be worth about 17 per cent less in April 2009 than it was in April 2008. If I were trying to sell it, that might bother me, although I would also know that most other houses would have fallen by a similar amount. But I am not trying to sell it, and so who cares? Of course, being a housing academic, I have been asked by several people – friends, family, the engineer servicing our central heating boiler – whether they should try to sell their house. Unlike the exhortations of government ministers, I do not see it as my civic duty to encourage people to spend, and so my advice tends to be that it might be best to wait a while unless a move is really unavoidable. But I don't consider this to be rocket science and nor was this why I did my PhD.

One consequence of the credit crunch has been to emphasise housing finance over housing itself. But, as I have argued in the Introduction, housing is not the same as finance. Whilst it is quite natural for us to concentrate on issues of finance in a financial crisis, we still need to remember that we can carry on using our housing pretty much as before. We might see that markets have failed and look at the huge levels of toxic debt on the balance sheets of the world's banks as proof. We could suggest that capitalism is at a crossroads and the end of the Reagan/Thatcher era of laissez-faire is at hand. We might argue for the nationalisation of more banks and the public lynching of bankers. But we still sit on the sofa in front of the TV to find out about all this, and we still lock the door and draw the curtains to close out the world when we choose to.

The view that most people have of markets, be they critics or supporters, tends to be quite fundamentalist. By this I mean there is an assumption that markets are at the centre of our considerations when it comes to housing. This, we might say, is the public face of housing in countries such as the UK and US. When housing is discussed, it is usually in terms of mortgage rates, foreclosures and repossessions, house price changes, and so on. Our discussions on housing are now all about numbers and abstractions, and the implication is that this is how we see housing: to talk about housing is to discuss prices and the levels of market activity.

But for most of us, most of the time, this is not what housing is about. Many, perhaps a majority, of us have not been near a housing market for years. Markets have an instrumental quality rather than being things in themselves. They are one of the forms of social relations that allow us to buy and sell things, such as houses. We need them because they are useful, but we do not need them all the time. We are glad that they are there, but only when we want them. We cannot control markets, but we can, to a certain extent, control when we use them. The reason that we use them is that markets work well enough most of the time and for most purposes. They are the most efficient and effective means of allocating scarce resources that human beings have been able to come up with. But this does not mean they are the very focus of our lives.

There is an inevitable tendency to focus attention on the difficulties that some households might have in terms of affording housing or gaining access to housing, and this will colour our view of markets. The danger of this, however, is that these situations will then be taken to be normal, typical and permanent. We might start to assume that market failure is inevitable and so government should intervene in housing markets. This view tends to forget that government already intervenes to a considerable extent (as we shall see in the next chapter), but it also gives the impression that markets fail always and for everyone. But of course they do not always fail. In most cases, and in most times, markets work tolerably well, and most people are perfectly capable of using them when they have to.

What I wish to do in this chapter is to consider how households actually relate to markets, rather than just assuming their centrality. This is not because I wish to suggest that markets do not work, or that they should be replaced by something else, but because we can understand the nature of housing boom and bust only if we can appreciate how we relate to markets. My approach is what might be called a phenomenological view of housing finance, which concentrates on how use creates meaning for our housing and how we can operationalise this using finance. This is an approach that does not rely on the economics of the household, although this is a perfectly valid approach to explaining family behaviour (Bryant and Zick 2006). Nor is this a study of the social relations associated with market behaviour, which again is a useful means of exploring the issues, as shown in the developing area of the microstructures of housing markets (Smith and Munro 2008a, 2008b). Likewise, I might have borrowed from the fascinating and developing area of using behavioural models to explain economic and social phenomena (Frey and Stutzer 2007; Ubel 2009) as well as being used to inform public policy (Thaler and Sunstein 2008)

One of my reasons for using this approach is that I have been motivated by the following question. What shall we have left after boom and bust is over? The answer to this question is both obvious and troubling. We shall have pretty much the same situation as we have now: a dominant owner-occupied sector, housing policy dictated by the desire to own and the need to use markets if we want to access housing. This is not meant to show any complacency, but just what alternative is there? In the UK in 2006 there were nearly 26.5 million dwellings of which 18.5 million or 70.1 per cent were in the owner-occupied sector (Wilcox 2008). We have to consider just what set of circumstances could possibly alter this dominance in the short to medium term.

The reason this answer is troubling is twofold. First, because it means that any fundamental change might be difficult, if not impossible. All we may be able to do is to return to where we were before, with only some minor changes at the margin. But second, it is troubling because it means that the issue is not one of policy design at all, but of attitudes and how we presume to engage with markets. My argument in the later chapters of this book is that government in particular has seriously misunderstood markets and the manner in which households engage with them. The result has been to confuse corporate interests with free market activity. This has created a series of perverse incentives based on the interests of government, larger corporations and households. One way of preventing this occurring again, along with changes in the way government regulates and intervenes in markets, is for us to understand more fully how individuals relate to housing markets. This is why in this chapter we explore individual behaviour with regard to finance and markets and only then shall we embark on an analysis of the financial crisis. In the first section of this chapter I consider the concept of really private finance, which I use to explore the way in which individuals relate to markets. This leads to a discussion of what it means to be involved in markets and how this links in with our expectations and aspirations.

## Really private finance

Our continued relationship with the financing of our dwelling, despite its importance, tends to be rather distant. Practically it is most likely that we make monthly mortgage payments by a direct debit through our bank, and the only contact we have with our lender is through an annual statement of what we have paid and what we still owe. Of course there are other issues we need to attend to, such as paying bills and annual insurance renewals. We tend to deal with these in ways that are formal: by letter and through arrangements with banks again. If we are particularly modern, we might now make some of these arrangements on-line.

There is not any direct relationship with financial institutions. There is very little face-to-face contact after the initial mortgage has been negotiated and agreed. We might, from time to time, change our mortgage, set up a new fixed-rate arrangement, or change our energy supplier, but this is all done through formal administrative procedures. There is nothing that is intimate or close, and this applies even though finance is something we might treat as private and confidential.

This, however, is exactly how we wish the relationship over housing finance to be and precisely as it should be. We want a high degree of formality because this is more likely to ensure the security of our assets. But we have next to no expectations of our lender, other than that they treat us with competence, fairness and honesty. We want, and need, to have no further relationship with our mortgage lender or electricity supplier. We require a means to contact them and some means of redress if they fail in their obligations. We expect clarity in terms of what we shall be, and have been, charged and that the service they are contracted to provide will be delivered. Yet we expect no day-to-day contact, and so they remain distant. We continue to live in the dwelling, the lights come on, water comes out of the taps and the bins are emptied. All we need to do is pay the bills.

And, as long as we maintain the payments and pay our bills, we shall not be bothered. The cycles go on; there is a regularity in terms of the relationship with these agencies. We make our regular payments and in return we can continue with our lives free from interference. Of course mortgage lenders and energy companies can influence what we do, most particularly if prices rise. If mortgage payments or energy bills increase, we might have to alter our behaviour. But, despite this, the relationship with these bodies is a formal one. These companies do not seek to improve us or control us. They merely wish us to pay our bills on time. This is the main condition of the relationship: we pay what we owe and in return they supply us with a service. All our mortgage lender is interested in is the contractual relationship between us and they are content to leave us alone. We can be identified only by a code or reference number and, despite attempts to personalise their service and emphasise the importance of good manners, we expect and respect this level of formality, which we see as guaranteeing a degree of competence and certainty.

These formal relations exist to provide us with something that is very intimate. The finance supports the activity of dwelling, whereby we are able to sustain, care for and protect ourselves and those close to us. Indeed, our dwelling – the place where we live – is itself something that is very close to us. We operate within it. It wraps us up and encloses us. The dwelling allows us to include those we love and to exclude all others. It acts as a barrier that is physical and psychological. We are close to it because of what it allows us to do, what it prevents, particularly ingress of the unwanted, but also because of what it means to us. It is our personal place, where we can care and share without inhibition (King 2004, 2005, 2008).

The virtue of our private dwelling is that it allows us to be secure and complacent about our surroundings and our place in the world. We might see complacency as a vice, as a way of ignoring the world around us, or not facing up to the world as it is, but rather seeking to take things only on our terms. Yet this is precisely why the dwelling is so significant to us. We need some place where we can be free of the expectations of others and where we relax and act only with regard to our intimates. The privacy and security of private dwelling, which prevents unwanted others from impinging upon us, allows for this complacency (King 2003, 2005, 2008). This sense of private dwelling, of course, is something shared by most households.

What private dwelling provides us with is regularity and this returns us to the financial basis of our housing. Our financial affairs may be formal and perhaps somewhat distant, but they are cyclical and are based on a regularity of actions and commitments. These formal relations provide us with patterns of consistency, which allow only for slow and predictable change. This allows us not only to plan, but also to continue within our complacency. Once we have set up our financial relations – our standing orders, so to speak – we need not do much more. We can run on autopilot without worrying about dramatic changes or whether we can maintain our lifestyle. If we wish to take a risk, we can do and we shall have a base from which to leap. The stability of our base allows us to change and commit to new opportunities in a manner that would not be possible were the stability not present beneath us. But, because of that support, we need not take the risk.

When we talk of regularity we think of precise intervals and of repetition. Regularity, of course, is the noun derived from regular, which we can see as referring to what is normal, customary, usual and expected. It allows processes to develop according to a uniform principle, or occur at fixed or pre-arranged intervals. When things are regular, they follow a set rule or practice. To be regular is to be a creature of habit, one who is consistent and who follows established patterns of behaviour. We see such people as being dependable and efficient and as those who perhaps have a balanced view of their place in the world. They may be somewhat formal, but this can be a virtue when dealing with finance or impersonal relations. Particularly important for our discussion here is the sense that regularity has of depending on the expected and what is normal. If we can establish regularity, there are no surprises, but rather patterns and predictability. This allows us to feel secure and stable, that we are not in a precarious position or under threat. We can take our situation for granted in the belief that contingencies are taken care of. There is a sense in which we can accept our environment and our place in it and feel that we belong (King 2008). We do not have to strive particularly to achieve our ends, but feel that we are close to them. It is where we are comfortable, not just in the material sense, but in the existential sense of knowing our place within the world (King 2005).

Regularity, therefore, allows for the existential and the financial to be brought together.

I wish to refer to this manner in which we can underpin the existential, and create regularity, as really private finance. I shall use the term to relate to the level of activity that centres on individual decision-making and individual relationships concerning housing. It is a term that need not be reserved for housing, although the nature of housing is such that there is always likely to be a direct financial relationship with bodies external to the household, unlike those goods that are provided by the state free of charge, such as education and health care.

But I also want to use the term really private finance precisely because not all the cost of housing, for some households at least, is met from their own resources. Housing is open to public policy intervention and government provides finance to support the production and consumption of housing. So housing finance is an arena of government action, and this alters the nature of private activity (King 2009). The issue of public finance is therefore an important one.

Accordingly, there is a more knowing and ironic meaning to the use of the term 'really private finance' and, in particular, the word 'really': this is because of the importance to housing, and public provision in particular, of what has become known as 'private finance'. Since the end of the 1980s successive governments have engineered a situation in which new social provision can be built only with a significant private contribution. Public grants are limited to a fixed proportion of the capital cost and the residue must be raised by private borrowing. In addition, since 1990, over a million council dwellings have been transferred to housing associations, meaning that private finance is also now used to improve and maintain the stock.

Government housing policy depends on private finance, and the levels of activity could not be maintained without it. Private finance is used to offset public expenditure and is managed in such a way that government retains control over systems whilst minimising its financial liabilities. Government seeks to pass the risk over to private institutions in exchange for a reasonable rate of return. But government still maintains bureaucratic control over the housing (King 2009).

This means that what we have come to refer to as private finance is actually glaringly public. The term private finance is always used in relation to public policy and to public projects. It is a means of funding state-sponsored projects without government having to commit to the expenditure itself. Hence we have seen an increasing use of the so-called Private Finance Initiative (PFI) as a means of funding public projects through the private sector and paying for these through long-term revenue funding.

Private finance is used to fund public projects and it is being defined by government as a means of meeting its policy objectives. Indeed, as was shown recently by the failure of Metronet, a PFI company involved in improving the London Underground, government has had to underwrite these activities. It is simply unrealistic for large-scale public infrastructure, such as the capital's underground system, to fail as a result of a particular funding mechanism. In 2009 the British government had to intervene and provide funding for several PFI projects that were struggling to achieve the requisite private funding. Accordingly, we now have the thorough-going absurdity of a publicly funded Private Finance Initiative.

Private finance is controlled by government and has a specific public function. It has developed as a top-down process to suit government priorities, particularly the need to control public expenditure whilst increasing or maintaining outputs. Private finance has been initiated therefore out of public processes to achieve public ends, and has not arisen out of the operation of private organisations or through spontaneous actions. So private finance is actually a public policy mechanism. We might say, therefore, that it is somewhat unreal.

In contrast really private finance is about what individuals do with their own money, in their own time, to meet their own ends. It is the use of finance for private purposes, and it very much pre-dates the use of private finance as a public policy mechanism. Really private finance should be seen as a concern for bottom-up processes, initiated by individual households taking decisions based on the circumstances in which they find themselves. Really private finance is about how we use our own money to meet our own needs, wants and aspirations. Quite clearly these actions can have a public impact in aggregate, and government can seek to use fiscal and monetary policy to try to affect the behaviour of individuals. But government does not initiate these actions, and they do not arise out of government's purposes. Governments may involve themselves in income maintenance and, of course, they tax the income of individuals. But it is not generally seen as the role of government to direct the expenditure of individuals. Indeed modern governments do not see it as their role to ensure income equality, even if they might seek to ensure a minimum income.

Generally speaking, we are assumed to be able to use our income as we please, and this is the sense in which I use the term really private finance. How we use our income is no concern of anyone but ourselves. The outcomes of this use are our problem and our responsibility. Any benefit that accrues is ours, and any loss falls on us too. What we are concerned with, therefore, is those decisions we make and which only we can properly make (and still have income to control). Really private finance is about how we use our resources for our own purposes, on the basis of our definition of our purposes and in our own time and in our own way.

What concerns me here is not how we gain the income, but how we use what we have. So once an individual is given income support through a government scheme, it becomes theirs and is really private. Government recognises this basic principle through the use of income maintenance schemes rather than through the use of food and clothing vouchers. Interestingly, it is now UK government policy to make Housing Benefit payments directly to claimants rather than allowing the subsidy to be paid to their landlord. The justification for this change is the need to build personal responsibility by ensuring that tenants pay their own rent. They should be able to manage their own responsibilities and this can be done through having control over a personal income as is the case for those individuals who earn their own income (DWP, 2002). The drift in welfare policy appears to be moving towards personal responsibility and the idea, therefore, that we all have access to really private finance.

For the majority of households this is already the case, in that what we achieve is through the use of our own income on the basis of the plans we have devised and tried to implement. This is not a perfect situation, since there may be a considerable gap between our aspirations and our achievements. Nevertheless, what we do achieve is the result of our own initiative.

The importance of the concept of really private finance is more significant than merely as a critique of government housing and welfare policies. The concept, I believe, is very important in teasing out the manner in which we can and do use our housing and the way in which we want or aspire to do so. It helps us get to the heart of the relationship between our dwelling and ourselves as thinking, acting beings who are capable of setting goals and deciding on a means of achieving them. Really private finance helps clarify for us the possibilities and limits that surround us in the dwelling. It demonstrates to us what we can and cannot do. By putting an emphasis both on our own resources and what we wish to use them for, it brings into clear focus what we are able to do with the dwelling, and what the dwelling allows us to do. It enables us to state what it is that we must do for ourselves and what cannot be done by anyone but ourselves. Really private finance, being concerned with the use of our resources within the sphere of our own private actions, focuses on our responsibilities and the limitations this may place on us. It takes as a given that we have responsibilities for our family and the upkeep of the dwelling itself and helps to demonstrate the centrality of these relations.

It also shows that the most private sphere is linked into markets and the wider social whole, even at the global level. Our income – our really private finance – is derived from the external world of employment, and government policy and practice. We are therefore at the mercy of the external world to some extent. We may have some insulation from external influence because of our savings and the assets we hold, or because we can rely on the resources of others, such as our parents. Alternatively, we may find ourselves in exactly the right circumstances for particular market conditions, for instance, a small mortgage relative to the value of our house and income, and so we are not affected markedly once housing markets decline. But whatever the specific case, the insulation we might have is never total and sooner or later we shall have to face up to the limitations of market conditions and government action.

An appreciation of our own resources and the expectations we have of them and of our dwelling environment might help us to understand why we do not need intervention when we are comfortable, but also what intervention is for once we, or others, have too few resources. This, at one level, might appear to be an obvious point – rich people can look after themselves, but poor people cannot – yet the reality is rather more complex, as we can quite readily see when we begin to consider not just income levels, but the issues of commitments and expectations. Do we expect our situation to improve or worsen, and what leeway do we have to cope if it worsens? Is our family increasing in size – more mouths to feed – or decreasing because our children have left home? Can we reasonably expect our income to rise over time and so might we be able to afford a bigger mortgage? Is there a reasonable prospect of house price inflation? What are our priorities and interests regarding how we live? How capable are we of deciding our own affairs, and what happens if – or when – this changes?

This combination of income, aspirations, expectations and decision-making capability starts to show the complexity of our housing situation and why it is not simply sufficient to concentrate on one factor, such as income. In other words, it properly personalises the relationship between finance and housing in a manner that goes beyond the generalities normally associated with the subject of housing finance. It stresses that we do not merely respond to financial stimuli.

The concept of really private finance is important in that it starts to regulate and determine the role of other agencies we relate to, and consequently puts the work of these agencies into some perspective. By making clear what opportunities and limits there are to our own income, choices and aspirations, it questions what roles government and other agencies might have. It helps to state what government and other agencies cannot, and must not, do if they are to allow us to dwell privately, and what forms of intervention are legitimate. By stating the proper relations between private dwelling and finance – by making clear what is really private – we can start to see what we can do for ourselves and thus where the potential gaps are. But, importantly, the determination of what is legitimate and where the limits are is not formed entirely externally, but as a result of the relationship between our housing and our income, current circumstances and aspirations. The concept of really private finance, therefore, can provide us with a helpful bottom-up approach to understanding the complexities of dwelling as lived experience.

We need to appreciate that finance may not be at the heart of our decision-making. We might not make a decision solely on financial grounds, but rather rely on finance as the enabler or facilitator of our needs and aspirations. It is all too easy for those whose primary interest is finance to forget that housing finance is a means and not an end in itself (King 2009). It might be that financial considerations impinge only at certain times. Obviously this would be when we need to buy or sell a dwelling, but it will also be when housing markets are in recession and we become anxious about the value of our dwelling or increases in our housing costs. It is clear that if we are in debt and struggling to repay our mortgage, then housing finance will loom very large in our consciousness. But then not all of us will react in the same manner. Some people may be more sanguine about debt than others, and see it as a sustainable position. Others might hide from the issue and refuse to deal with it, on the basis that something might turn up or that they may never have to face the problem.[1] So some people may not even consider finance – their mortgage or rent arrears – even when they clearly ought to.

We perhaps see finance as something of a mystery, as something we use only when we have to. Most of us, most of the time, are sufficiently comfortable that we have a considerable margin, which allows us to ignore finance, or rather to take it

---

1 I deal with this issue of hiding from responsibility in *In Dwelling* (King 2008).

for granted. We do not need to understand how financial markets work and, unless we are faced with a crisis, we do not even notice how ignorant we are. All we need to be aware of is how much we are paying and for how long.

I do not see this as financial incompetence or ignorance. It is not that we do not understand something important. Instead it is a case of the complacency that comes from regularity. We have made our payments consistently and see no reason why we shall not continue to do so into the future. We do not believe we have anything to worry about because we feel, based on our experience, that our housing is affordable. We expect that we can carry on as before and that the financial arrangements will be consistent and predictable. When this situation alters so will our perception of housing finance. This might lead us to suggest that we should all become 'financial experts' once we are faced with a threat to our complacency. The near collapse of world financial markets and the steep decline in house prices since 2007 has heightened our awareness of housing finance to the extent that US mortgage institutions like Fannie Mae and Freddie Mac feature on the UK national news. When house prices were rising and households felt more affluent, they had no need to understand the workings of mortgage lenders, from where they sourced their finance and what the implications of these were. But now, after the failure of Bradford & Bingley and Northern Rock in the UK, this has become a very important political issue.

By focusing on the personal level, we can start to appreciate the impact of changes at the macro level and the manner in which we might, or might not, respond at the micro level. If we have a reasonable income and a relatively small mortgage compared to the value of our dwelling we might not alter our behaviour. But if we had just bought a property and mortgaged ourselves up to the limit in the expectation that the good times would continue, we might have to drastically reduce our discretionary expenditure and may well fear that our housing would become unaffordable, or that we could not afford to sell the house because of the loss we would incur.

This does not mean that finance is everything, even when we find ourselves in difficulties. As John Turner (1976) has argued, we need to differentiate between the economic and human values of housing. We need to remember that housing has an existential significance – it binds us to our environment and allows us to fulfil our ends – and it can do this without regard to the material value of the dwelling, or even, Turner argues, without necessarily any direct correlation to material standards and amenities. A dwelling still fulfils the same function for us as needful human beings whether it is valued at £180,000 or falls to £150,000. We can use it in the same manner on a day-to-day basis. Indeed, even if we are in mortgage arrears, the dwelling shelters and protects us. Of course it will not continue to do so indefinitely, and we shall be forced to act to remedy the situation, but this does not alter the basic qualities offered by the dwelling.

So Turner argues for a distinction between the existential and economic values of the dwelling, and we shall discuss this again later in the chapter. However, for now we should see that there is a connection between the existential and the economic. Indeed, the fact that we have to pay for the dwelling demonstrates this link at the most basic level. This connection is not necessarily straightforward or simple to understand. We might see the existential and economic as two sides of the same coin. It is precisely the virtue of the concept of really private finance – that it joins use and expectations with resources and so links the existential and economic into one practical conception – that allows us to make sense of this connection. Really private finance allows us to see the connection as well as the distinction between the activity of dwelling and its material value, both as an object in itself and in terms of its economic significance as an object connected to the external world.

The determining factor in really private finance is personal decision-making or, rather, how our personal-decision making relates to general external factors. The importance of housing finance to us is, to a considerable extent, dependent upon our actions. We are of course affected by external factors, such as global markets and government action, and we can have little control over these. But we need to remember that the operation of these external factors is nearly always general. Changes in market conditions are not directed at particular individuals or groups, but have their effect because of the specific situation that individuals or groups find themselves in. Again, even though government action might be more targeted than market activity, it is still general and its impact is dependent on the specific situation of the individual or group. So markets and governments act in a general way and how they impact is dependent on the specific situations in which individuals find themselves. These situations derive from the actions individuals have taken and the choices they have made.

So, for example, a household might have mortgaged themselves to the hilt and left themselves with no leeway if interest rates rise. Another household might have been cautious and maintained a relatively small mortgage. In this way these households are either prepared or unprepared to meet changes over which they have no control, such as an economic downturn, higher interest rates, stagnant real-term income growth, and so on. We may indeed see these latter issues as the real problems, and they will certainly cause considerable difficulties to some households. Yet this does not detract from the overall point that an individual household's situation is dependent on the choices they have made in terms of house purchase. We are therefore always, in part, culpable in terms of what happens to us.

It might be argued that some households have no alternative. The shortage of available dwellings to rent and their inability to access social housing mean that some households have no alternative but to buy a property, and to do this they borrow heavily and, perhaps in hindsight, recklessly. This being so, how can they be held responsible for changes in housing markets, which make their situation unsustainable? Any answer to this question will have the tendency to sound either glib or unsympathetic, or perhaps even both. However, this situation is precisely why an understanding of really private finance is so important. No one who purchases a dwelling, regardless of the pressure they feel they are facing, can reasonably have done so under actual duress. Households are not forced to buy any particular dwelling. However, it is doubtless the case that some households feel they have no alternative but to buy an expensive dwelling in London. Yet most people need not live in London, but do so because of family connection, employment or other lifestyle reasons. These are all entirely valid on their own terms, and it would be impertinent for anyone to question them, but it does not mean that the household is forced to stay in the most expensive city in the country.

So why do people do it? S has lived in Cambridge for over 30 years and she likes it there. Her job is there, she has many friends and finds much about the city to enjoy and relish. Yet Cambridge is one of the most expensive cities in Britain. House prices are double what they are in Peterborough, her home town, just 40 miles away. As she is not in a particularly highly paid job the cost of housing in Cambridge has been a constant issue. She now lives in a former council house in one of the less leafy parts of the city. The house is fine for her and allows her to live in the city. Yet were she to sell up and move back to her home town, she could either buy a very smart detached house, or save herself a lot of money in housing costs. But she doesn't and she won't. Partly this is because of work, but it is mainly because of friends, her established lifestyle and what has become habitual and normal for her; if you like, it is what makes her life worthwhile. This includes things like her friends, the many little pubs, the madrigals by the river in the college gardens, the college bumps, cycling past King's College chapel every day, the arts cinema and just the vibrancy of life in this particular city. What matters most to S is not the cost of housing. Of course this is important and has caused her some worry, but this is not the overriding factor. She feels she belongs in Cambridge. She is used to living there and is prepared to do what she needs to maintain her life there. This is the essence of her life and the practical considerations of housing costs begin from this point.

S, like most people, believes that she should be able to live where she pleases, and it is not for others to say she should not, and she is all too aware of the consequences which flow from this. She has certain expectations which motivate her behaviour, and which preclude her from taking other decisions, such as moving to Newcastle or Swansea. This is entirely a matter for her and so is what follows as a result. The same applies to anyone who stays in an expensive area when, objectively, there are alternatives. Subjective considerations which are immune to precise calculation or generalisation keep them in that place.

This subjectivity, however, does not mean that the community as a whole or the government is beholden to support them. We hope that, like S, people take decisions in the full knowledge of the consequences that might ensue and that the benefits outweigh the costs. But this does mean that they are responsible for their situation and they should bear the consequences of their decisions.

Indeed the way in which we expect government to act serves to reinforce this understanding that our predicament is self-made. We might accept that bank deposits should be guaranteed by government, at least up to a certain amount,[2] but we do not believe that it should guarantee the value of our house. Nor do we think that it is improper for a lender to seek repossession if we default on the mortgage. Whilst we would not want this action taken against ourselves or those we know, or even enjoy the prospect of it happening to anyone, we can see that it is a necessary part of how markets work. We realise what the consequences would be if there were no sanction against mortgage defaulters.

In a housing recession we might expect government to act and use fiscal and monetary policy to effect a recovery in housing markets. We might also accept that there may be the need for emergency measures in some extreme circumstances. But we do not expect government to become involved in individual cases. Instead, like much of government action, the intervention should be general rather than on a case-by-case basis.

An individual is presumed to be in control of their finances and to be competent to pay their bills and meet their responsibilities. They are deemed able to make choices and to be aware of the consequences. We assume a degree of personal responsibility and culpability on the part of individuals, and consequently we believe that they must bear at least some of the

---

2   In October 2008 the UK government increased its savings guarantee from £35,000 to £50,000, whilst several European governments offered 100 per cent guarantees.

responsibility for their financial difficulties; this applies even when we might agree that a person really has just been unlucky and has done very little wrong if, for example, they chose to buy an expensive house just as the market was turning. Households can suffer from bad luck, but this does not mean that they should be cushioned from the impact of their ill-luck. The problem is that we cannot, or find it very difficult, to separate out the ill-luck from the bad decision, and these from the deliberate act of omission or reckless decision. We also might believe that providing for these cases will encourage reckless behaviour and acts of omission (King 2000; Murray 1984).

Perhaps a more pertinent reason is that we just do not believe it is anyone else's business to interfere in the private affairs of an individual. We have taken a decision based not on the general good, but on our own interests. This is in itself perfectly normal. However, it does mean that we cannot expect society to support us. We do not seek to take property (or most of it, at least) away from those who are just lucky or have shown good judgement in accumulating wealth, and also we do not feel we should bail out those who are unlucky or have shown poor judgement. This is simply taken as a proper consequence of personal decision-making.

For government to actually deal with ill-luck would involve a tremendous amount of intervention and arbitrary assumptions on what constitutes good and bad luck, and what is the legitimate scope for personal decision-making. We can see a link here with Nozick's thought experiment on perfect equality, his 'Wilt Chamberlain' case, in which government has to reallocate income even though all transfers have been voluntary (Nozick 1974). Nozick describes a hypothetical society of perfect income equality. However, many individuals are prepared to pay a voluntary premium to watch a particularly talented basketball player, Wilt Chamberlain. At the end of the basketball season Chamberlain has a considerably higher income than the rest of the society, but this has arisen entirely out of voluntary acts taken by individuals aware of what they were doing. Nozick argues that income equality could be maintained only by considerable and continuous intervention by government that would run counter to the voluntary decisions of individuals who have taken great pleasure in watching an exceptional player.

Likewise for government to involve itself in dealing with individual cases of ill-luck would involve an absurd and impractical level of intervention and forced transfers. It would effectively involve the nationalisation of the housing stock and its general allocation through some central uniform and standard procedure. It would also exonerate any individual of any culpability for the situation they find themselves in and create a considerable moral hazard, whereby the incidence of the undesired outcome would increase. If we were aware that we would not have to bear the consequences of our action, we might well behave in an irresponsible and arbitrary manner. The fact that we know we shall have to accept the consequences of what we have done is an important element in making rational decisions. Without personal responsibility we could act with impunity and effectively become infantilised.

This is an important element in how we relate to markets. We know that we have to take the consequences of our decisions and this motivates how we act. So, with this in mind, how do markets look from an individual's point of view?

## Going off to market

We do not talk about going off to market any more. Our ancestors, knowing there was only one place to buy and sell things, might have done, but we do not tend to. We might see a market as something that exists – that there actually is such a thing – but not in any concrete sense any more. We may still visit a street market and are likely to use a supermarket, but still the market is something that is vaguely 'out there'. We see it as a loose collection of shops, firms, other households, and so on. But whilst we might say we are going shopping, or off to Sainsbury's, we do not tend to say that we are now going to participate in market activities. Likewise, we might think that we need to move house, but we would not consider this as joining the housing market.

Of course we might idly browse in shop windows and buy something on impulse (although perhaps not a house), but acting on impulse still means that the buying is purposive. We switch from passive – just browsing – to active and interested. Something catches our eye and we decide we want it and that there is really nothing to stop us from having it. It is at that moment that it becomes important: when 'I want' shifts to 'I can' or 'There is nothing to stop me'. However, we do not say that we are now consuming, or that we are participating in the market.

Some people do speculate on markets, including the one for property, and doubtless enjoy it. They might even make a career of it, and so see this as an end in itself. But still, is this not about the rewards or the thrill of risk-taking rather than market participation? Is it not the wealth or the risk that matters in the end rather than the processes involved? The processes are necessary and it might be fun, but is this really what people do it for?

For most of us markets are things we hear about, whereas we just buy things when we want them. Does this then mean that the market is an abstraction or even a metaphor for something else? Certainly we can see it as just a way of describing a particular set of social relations based on the exchange of rights over property. We can also see the market as an aggregate of transactions and relations. We might, of course, talk about a particular market and still mean our local street market. But when we use the term, it does not have to refer to a particular place. A market need not be limited or closed; it is not necessarily geographically bounded or contiguous.

We might even say that any particular definition or sense of what markets are is not particularly relevant. What motivates us is the specific good or service that we require at that point in time and the conditions needed to attain it. Often these conditions need little in the way of preplanning. We go out for a drink, buy a bar of chocolate, choose a new tie, or buy a book having read the blurb on the back. These need no preplanning or deep thought, and this is simply because we have the money and anyway the level of expense involved is relatively small. Our decisions depend even here on a number of factors, such as the level of our income, where we choose to go for a drink and how important we consider our attire to be and thus how much we are prepared to spend on the tie.

There may well not be any consistency here. I spend an inordinate amount of money on books, and I have on at least two occasions spent more than £100 on a single book. However, I doubt that I could be persuaded to spend more than £10 on a bottle of wine in a supermarket. Likewise, my father-in-law would happily go for a drink with his friends after a round of golf, but he would not buy a meal in the pub. He would wait until he got home on the grounds that they had plenty of food in the house. But if the aim was economy, why not save some more money and get the beers from the supermarket and invite his friends over? The reason, of course, was that he went out to meet his friends and not just for the drinking. Still, an inconsistency remained, much to the amusement of his wife and daughters. So we tend to exhibit certain priorities and choices which may not be particularly rational.

As individuals we have different priorities in terms of what we consider to be value for money, or a reasonable use of our income. We therefore might not be maximising our income in any objective sense. We might not be spending our money to our best advantage and this could be because of ignorance, infirmity or even a relative lack of money itself. People who depend on a pension or welfare benefits may have to buy their food from corner shops in relatively small quantities on a daily basis rather than being able to do a large shop at a supermarket every fortnight or month and so take advantage of bulk buying or special offers. Supermarket buying is cheaper in the long term than using corner shops, but one needs the money to be able to do this.

Other people will spend far more on a car than they objectively need to. This is because they really like driving or because they want a particular sort of vehicle in terms of its look, speed, engine capacity, status, etc. We can question how many people actually need an SUV to negotiate supermarket car parks, but this is their choice. Also why do people buy expensive mobile phones when they could just as readily speak to their friends on a basic model, and why buy a £7,000 watch, when they could purchase a perfectly good watch for £50? Part of this decision-making may be due to marketing, or to the deliberate inculcation of a particular image. But most important is the simple fact that people are able to and choose to act on this. In these circumstances, we might ask why they should not. People make choices based on the resources they have, on what they consider to be a priority. They consider the expense to be necessary or justifiable. It is their money they are spending, and if they are harming no one in the process, we might argue that it is no one else's business.

Of course much of our spending is not discretionary, but is fixed according to our particular circumstances. We have certain commitments that have arisen as a result of decisions we have taken in the past. These decisions might not have been well thought out or the full ramifications considered, but once we have made that choice we are stuck with it and this will determine what we spend our money on. Accordingly, if we fall in love with the little country cottage and decide to buy it, we may then find that we need to drive everywhere. Obviously, if we buy a house, we need to maintain it and we have to pay our bills. If we wish to use our car, we must fill it with fuel and make sure it is taxed and insured.

But we do address markets differently and this psychology towards the use of money is fascinating. A particularly interesting example, for me at least, is the markedly different behaviour of my two daughters. This is a useful example precisely because they are not currently financially independent and so all their expenditure is discretionary and led by their choices and impulses. They are fed, clothed and sheltered by their parents and so they can spend their money on what they want. My eldest daughter has no trouble in spending what money she has. But her sister is the precise opposite. She gets embarrassed when she has accumulated what she considers to be too much money and banks it so it is out of mind. She finds it hard when people wish to treat her and spend money on her without good reason: this means anything beyond what she strictly needs and what she is given at Christmas and on her birthday. Even here she cavils at excess. She will buy things on occasion and, strictly speaking, they will not be necessary. But often when I tell her I want to buy her something, her response is to say that she simply does not need anything. I tell her not to worry about need, does she want anything? I go through a list – clothes, CDs, DVDs, books, shoes – but I know that she will just shake her head with a little uncomfortable smile, as if she is letting me down. And I know that when I offer to treat her elder sister, I shall be trailed around clothes and shoe shops for several hours waiting for her to narrow down the possibilities to the one key item she really cannot live without.

Now both these girls really lack for very little. Their parents are both employed, have a reasonable income and are able to give them all they need and most of what they want. They are not, I hope, spoiled, but the house is full of books, CDs, DVDs and old toys, many now neglected. But even though we treat them equally and they share much of what they have, they have very different attitudes towards material things and money. My elder daughter has mentioned that sometimes she wishes she had as much money as her sister. But then she reminds herself that she has had as much, but has spent it, and she can console herself with the things she has bought. This cheers her up and she returns to her books and her iPod. Her sister's situation is that she just cannot think of anything to spend her money on and shopping is dull and boring. She too much prefers to nestle up with a book or visit her friends.

Neither of these positions is extreme or in any way unhealthy. Being at school and financially dependent on their parents means they can get used to money in a relatively safe environment with a lot of leeway. They need not yet bear the full consequences of their actions. Neither can we say that one is right and the other wrong, at least not in any objective sense. But this attitude towards money held by two siblings is a fascinating example of how we differ not just in our propensity to choose, but even in our preparedness to choose. Both girls start with the same amount of money, but one could spend it twice or more, whilst the other has no idea what to do with it.

The importance of this example, and the discussion more generally, is that it starts to show how we face markets. We have different attitudes towards spending that may depend on our available income, but which is also conditioned by more imponderable issues. For some of us, spending our money is an enjoyable activity, but for others it is a chore to be avoided, unless absolutely necessary. We make different choices regardless of the state of the market, which might not be objectively rational but are rather discretionary and immune to generalisation. We can explore this further by looking at the complex issue of how our expectations and aspirations affect the way we address markets.

## Expectations

Much of our behaviour depends on what we expect to happen. As Akerlof and Shiller (2009) have shown, there has been a longstanding debate in economics regarding the role of expectations and whether individual economic actors act rationally. They argue that the neo-classical consensus built around Milton Friedman's work on expectations suggests that people can factor in economic phenomena, such as inflation, into their decision-making. In other words, they are able to take account of their expectations in a rational manner. Akerlof and Shiller, however, dispute this and seek to return to a Keynesian position that stresses that individuals can be fooled by money illusion and so ignore the impact of inflation and real-term changes in economic data.

Whatever the rights and wrongs of this debate, it is clear that the role played by expectations is important. In particular it is significant in the manner in which it relates to the idea of opportunity cost. Why are we prepared to forgo current expenditure or spending on other goods in order to fund our housing? Why are we prepared to pay so much for a particular dwelling, even if it involves struggling financially? We might argue that we are prepared to do this because of expectations of house price increases, which will lead to a considerable capital gain. It might also be that we feel that our income will increase relative to our housing costs and so our housing becomes more affordable in time.

Expectations are ours: we own them, in that they derive from, and belong to, particular individuals. I expect particular things and this might affect the manner in which I behave and how I react to particular stimuli. However, we cannot necessarily control our expectations. This is because they tend to be aimed at things beyond us. We have expectations of things that are outside of ourselves and beyond our control. We expect house prices to rise, but we have no direct means of affecting this trend. Therefore we might say that we do not actually own our expectations, rather they own us. We might see our housing as a store of wealth, which provides security for ourselves and our children. This wealth might provide us with additional consumption opportunities through equity withdrawal. We might expect this increase in wealth to continue indefinitely into the future. Akerlof and Shiller (2009) argue that there are many stories or narratives such as this, which state that house prices only rise and that therefore we cannot lose from investing in property. But we cannot control the nature of these increases and clearly not everyone can win from speculation: either some must lose so others can win at their expense, or there is a short-term bubble which then bursts to the detriment of most, as was the case in the UK and US between 2000 and 2009.

We tend to cast our expectations forwards, in that they influence our future behaviour. However, they depend on how we view our current and past situations. We have ambitions and hopes for the future. We might expect our wealth to increase and to pass this on to our children, but the basis on which we determine this is our current income and how it has altered in the past. Our expectations are based on what we can see has occurred in the past, which we then throw forward into the future on the assumption that this is part of a continuing trend.

But of course how we feel about the future affects how we act in the present. If we believe that house prices will continue to increase indefinitely into the future, we may bring forward a purchase or persuade ourselves to buy a more expensive property than we might otherwise have done if we believed that prices would remain static. This can work in reverse, such that if we feel prices will fall, we may delay a purchase until the bottom of the recession is reached to ensure we buy as cheaply as possible and avoid the problem of negative equity.

There is, therefore, an inevitable tension that exists between the present and the future. We may choose to forgo current consumption for some prospective future benefit. We can see this in economic or monetary terms, in that we have less money to spend now in the expectation of future gains. But we can also distinguish between the phenomenological and the financial: between the use we make of the dwelling and its economic value. There are meanings inscribed into the dwelling as the family home, the birthplace of our children, the centre of intimacy and a place of comfort and security (King 2004). But this has to be seen alongside the value of the dwelling, and how we react when we see that value increasing or decreasing, and the impact of medium- and long-term changes in our income. We cannot properly separate out the phenomenological and the financial, or the present from the future, but at different times one will pull us more strongly, with the effect that we may lose sight of the other facet.

The future, however, always has an advantage over the present, even if this advantage might turn out to be an illusion. The past and the present are known to us. We might not have a terribly accurate understanding of the past, but we can point to concrete actions and occurrences and we feel we can make categorical statements about what has already occurred. The future, by contrast, is full of possibility, and our expectations cannot be easily gainsaid by any inconvenient facts. An example of this distinction was seen in the case of housing in the UK between 2000 and 2006. The government claimed, entirely correctly, that housing was much cheaper in real terms than at any time in the last 40 years. This was due to lower interest rates and the increased competition caused by financial deregulation. However, the issue that increasingly dominated in the period was that of the rising unaffordability of housing. Housing costs may be lower than in the past, but the dominant story was of rapidly increasing house prices and a lack of supply. The government found itself having to respond to this story (CLG 2007; HM Treasury 2004); however, its claims of lower housing costs were largely ignored. The issue here was that individuals discounted the current situation – this was normal and so only to be expected

– and instead focused on what they saw as future trends. Instead of concentrating on current costs, they paid more attention to fears of increasing prices. Yet within a matter of two years UK households saw a rapid increase in housing costs in the first half of 2008 as the Bank of England increased interest rates, followed by a rapid fall in house prices and a collapse in the availability of mortgage finance. In mid-2009 it is impossible to argue that house prices will always rise. However, housing costs are now lower than ever with interest rates almost at zero. But it may not make us any more grateful towards the government to know that they were, technically speaking, right all along!

As the future is still full of possibility, we might be able to use it as a cushion or as a means to deal with our unsatisfactory present. But in doing so, we might prevent ourselves from actually changing our situation. If we are too full of expectations, we might not actually achieve anything at all. G is a woman who was divorced in the early 1980s by her husband, who was a relatively wealthy businessman. She now has little money compared to the amount she had been used to when she was married. However, she insisted on using what little she did have as if she were still relatively well off. She would spend her money in only two or three days and then go back, when she could, to using her credit card, always blaming others for the hard times she was now experiencing. Her views on money were very much like those of a young child being given a few pence in pocket money and going straight to the shop to spend it on sweets. There was an element of conspicuous consumption as well, as if spending a lot on something frivolous – a new hat or an expensive bottle of wine – was sending out a signal, even though she could not afford to do this consistently.

G seemed to live as if her current plight of little money – which had been going on for well over a decade – was actually temporary, and that she could get back 'out of the gutter' to the place where she felt she belonged. Therefore she was entitled to act as she did because having plenty of money was, by her account, her natural state, even though she made no real attempt to change her situation in order to realise her expectations. She made no attempt to find a job, never mind the highly paid one she would have needed to maintain her desired lifestyle. Rather G just seemed to expect this lifestyle as a matter of right, and so when she did have some money or the use of a credit card, she acted accordingly. This is a form of delusion, and a rather destructive one at that. But it does show the nature of expectations and attitudes and how they affect the way we behave. G's circumstances should have informed her that she was poor and that she should act accordingly. However, her 'dignity' would not allow her to claim welfare benefits – that apparently was what 'scroungers' did – but nor did she seek work until she absolutely had to. Rather she lived off a series of partners whilst she 'sorted' herself out, which sadly seemed to consist of finding someone to blame for her plight.

In time, when she found herself on her own, G had a series of low-paid jobs – factory work, care work – which was all she could find, not having worked for nearly 15 years. None of these jobs, however, allowed her to meet her aspirations. Indeed, her skills and work experience were such that there was very little she could do apart from low-paid work. Accordingly, there was a considerable mismatch between financial reality and G's self-image. She felt entitled to a lifestyle that demanded a middle-class income, which she had become accustomed to for a number of years before her divorce. Yet she did very little to achieve this and nor was she ever really able to regain her former lifestyle. However, she was apparently incapable of altering her expectations to meet her ongoing financial situation. We might suggest that there is something deeply troubling in this inability to connect with reality. The result of G's actions was serious debt, serial relationship breakdown and insecurity, with a seemingly ever heightening level of bitterness and recrimination. All of this could have been avoided if a more realistic view had been taken. Yet to G 'reality' was perhaps elsewhere, and the current and ongoing situation, even though it had lasted more than a decade, was a temporary aberration that would shortly end. She continued to assert that she had aspirations and a strong work ethic, despite all evidence to the contrary. She had a low opinion of those who were dependent on welfare benefits or on others, even while she lived off her partners. There was a high level of certainty about her delusions, an almost absurd mismatch between her sense of self and her actual situation, that was almost beyond parody.

Part of G's problem was being self-centred and looking at a particular far horizon to fulfil her own needs and aspirations. Undoubtedly, this was due to the serious hurt caused by her divorce and a feeling of being cheated by her ex-husband, who had effectively ruined her life. I say this, of course, having heard only her side of the story, but this is precisely the point: 'her side' is what this particular little story is about. The situation created by her divorce did not enable her to see beyond herself, and she had not the means to extract herself from this cycle of expectation and disappointment. G made no attempt to adapt to her current situation. She was always looking forward to when, so to speak, she would be back in her past and enjoying the status she considered was her right. There was no objective reason for her inability to change, especially as time went by and the knight on the white charger did not come to the rescue. But also there was seemingly nothing that could actually make her change.

So G maintained her aspirations even as she lived in a series of flats and bedsits, all of them temporary, because her luck was always about to change. She kept her belongings in boxes and bags, still packed. On one occasion she managed to get a flat she actually desired and which might be said to have been a considerable move up for her. This could have been the start of things turning round for her. However, G stayed there for only a year, never even having unpacked. Despite having aspired to live in this place for many years, she felt unable to invite anyone round because the living room was full of boxes and bags. She never got round to acquiring household essentials such as cutlery or an ironing board, and she kept the curtains drawn to prevent anyone seeing the state of the place. Yet, despite this, she still managed to invest in some very nice hats, always had wine in the flat and found the money to go out.

G's story consists of a series of rash and foolish financial decisions. We might see her as unworldly, but in the past she had successfully completed a university degree, held responsible jobs with internationally known companies and still, on her day, was good company. There was just this huge mismatch between who she wanted to be, or thought she was, and who she currently was. The result was a form of paralysis that prevented her from moving on, even though this appeared to be the very thing she most earnestly wished to do.

G's situation is certainly not a typical case, and we might argue that there is little to learn from such an extreme example. However, what G's behaviour shows with great clarity is the manner in which we relate to the future as a source of possibility and how we use the past selectively to help us. G's expectations paralysed her; they prevented her from progressing and developing in a realistic manner. The present was always contingent whilst her expectations were concrete.

The real tragedy about G's life was that her behaviour actually militated against her achieving her aspirations. She would not, or could not, settle and so found no stability. She therefore had nothing to build on, but was constantly looping back to her position of solitary insecurity. We might say that her problem was that she aspired in a manner that was unrealistic and was unachievable. However, it might be that it was these aspirations that made her life more bearable. If she truly had nothing to look forward to, she might have despaired completely. But, at the same time, she was holding on to what were completely unworldly expectations about her future.

G often found herself in debt, but she seemed to feel that this was a better position to be in than acting beneath the status she thought she ought to have. The debt was therefore a side-effect of what she saw as necessary to maintain some semblance of respectability. This situation offers an interesting entree into the issue of mortgage debt and how we view it. Most owner occupiers have a mortgage but would not consider themselves to be in debt. They tend to distinguish between a mortgage and other forms of debt, like a bank overdraft or credit card debt. This may be because of the value of the asset they are purchasing with the mortgage, which for many will now have grown to be in excess of their debt. Yet this is something of a false security in that values, as we have seen since 2006, can fall as well as rise, and if households need to liquidate their assets, they still need somewhere to live.

Despite this, mortgage debt is seen quite differently from other forms of debt and credit. In post-war Britain it was the accepted norm to borrow as much as one could possibly afford in order to buy a house in the expectation that the value of the house would increase and that earnings would rise, whilst repayments stayed relatively static. Therefore one would be paying out a diminishing proportion of one's income to pay for an appreciating asset. This applied only to housing, and the attitude towards other forms of debt was much less supportive. Akerlof and Shiller (2009) see this as an example of money illusion, in that one's view of appreciating values ignores the impact of inflation. The real-term increase in values is therefore rather lower than we imagine it to be.

This view about mortgage suggests that there is 'good' debt and 'bad' debt: the former is not problematical and is under control, while the latter has the potential for trouble. Yet we can only repay both from the same income stream, and it is the housing debt that is likely to dwarf the other forms, as well as being rather more long-term. In addition, other debt will often be at a fixed (although often higher) rate of interest so that the full cost is known in advance, whereas housing debt can fluctuate due to changing interest rates over the term of the loan.

Likewise we might suggest that there is 'good' spending and 'bad' spending, in terms of how we ought to prioritise our expenditure – for example, food, housing, clothing and fuel – as compared to more frivolous or inessential items. This applies particularly to households on low incomes. It might be assumed that they have little to fund discretionary expenditure or luxuries, but rather should be concentrating on necessities. However, the reality is that we do not tend to distinguish between necessities and luxuries, but rather between normal and abnormal expenditure based on our habits and expectations. As an example of this, I often ask my students – all of whom are mature and in full-time employment – how many of them really need a car. At the start most – 75–80 per cent at least – insist that they definitely do. However, I then challenge them about whether they really could not live without a car (I am a lifelong non-driver). I ask them whether they could not get another job if they wanted, or live somewhere else, or just manage with public transport or cycle, and eventually most – all but one or two – will agree that they could live, and live reasonably well, without one. There will be those who hold out and claim that they really do need one, and, for all I know, they may well be right.

When I ask how many of the students will now get rid of their car, none of them appears ready to do so. They do not want to give up their car, and this applies even when I ask if they are not concerned about the environment and global warming. They have no intention of forgoing the convenience of a car, and this is largely because they do not have to. Car driving is still legal and not penalised. Indeed, the fact that government taxes it and raises a considerable amount of revenue assures it of political support. They are only doing what everyone else is doing, and so, they suggest, why shouldn't they? Indeed they see me as doubly eccentric: first, for not driving myself and, second, for trying to tell them that they could manage without a car.

The key point here is that we do not often distinguish between what is essential and what is frivolous, and this is because we simply do not have to. Most of us can afford to have most of what we want and expect. The issue is therefore not about what is essential or inessential, but what is habitual and what we are used to. Most of us see the car as a habitual part of our lives and we have come to rely on it. It is now firmly part of our lifestyle and makes it possible to do many other things like shopping, day trips, holidays, ferrying the kids to and from places, and so on. Despite the complexity of the machine, it makes our lives simpler and easier, and so it becomes 'essential'. This situation is maintained largely because we are never challenged about what is or is not really necessary in our lives.

Most of what is around us – the technology, the entertainment, the things provided by markets and government – are not absolutely necessary. We could live without them, just as billions already do in less affluent parts of the world and as our ancestors managed to do. What is deemed essential is therefore as much to do with habit and our expectations of normality.

Our habitual actions are based on the regularity of complacency. This regularity is based on a lack of change. Many of the
key elements of our lives do not alter with any great frequency
and so we can maintain certain patterns. That much of our lives
is patterned allows us to maintain a lack of concern. We are not
constantly being surprised by events and we do not feel that
things are out of control. We might suggest that in this situation our expectations are within bounds. We are capable of
matching our expectations to the rhythms of our lifeworld. Our
expectations are in tune with the regularity that maintains us.

Returning to the case of G, we might suggest that her life can
be characterised not by a lack of regularity – a life could not be
lived without some forms of regular pattern, however fragmented
it might appear – but by the fact that the regularity does not
accord with her aspirations. Perhaps we should see this as a key
question. Are our aspirations and expectations matched by the
regularities of our life? G expected far more than she had or
would now be deemed realistic in the light of her circumstances.
She claimed to aspire, but really just expected it to happen at
some point; she expected that what she wanted would be just
handed to her. She should be allowed to live in the manner that
she expected and if she could not then this was unfair and
unreasonable. Others must be to blame for this, be it her ex-
husband, her current partner for holding her back, employers
who gave jobs to others, the state of the country or whatever.
But what was so important was that she could not, should not,
be held responsible for her situation. The fault for her condition
had to be located elsewhere because without this displacement
there could be no expectation of things ever getting better. If her
current condition was due to things she had either done or not
done then how could she escape, how could she retain her
dignity (and she had a lot), how could she keep her persona
together?

There is a form of fantasy here, a lack of reality. Yet G existed
in the all-too-real world, where things have prices attached
to them, where interest is charged and bills have to be paid by
the due date. This need for financial sense did not, however,
introduce itself fully into her consciousness. She would be down

when she had little or no money and no prospect of any. She would become bitter and depressed. Sometimes she would resent being 'kept', even as she took the money and blamed the person keeping her for holding her back. Once she had some money, she would be planning on what to spend it on, and it would all too quickly be gone. But she would accept no criticism of her behaviour, even from those she was largely dependent on. It was her money and she would use it how she wished. There was a high degree of stubbornness to this behaviour, but also a consistency, despite the lack of reality and common sense involved. She aspired to live like an upper-middle-class woman with an assumed artistic bent, yet she lived amongst unpacked boxes and cases and with the curtains drawn to prevent anyone seeing in, often refusing to answer the door to people. She had kept her skis, just in case!

The case of G shows that there is a tremendous unpredictability in the way in which people behave, and this might owe little to common sense notions of rationality. Indeed it is difficult to apply notions of rationality to expectations and aspirations, or rather we may do so only from the outside. We cannot achieve a rational engagement with someone such as G and expect her to be persuaded out of her destructive behaviour. Delving into the private hopes and ambitions of individuals is in any case fraught with difficulties. We are likely to cause offence and be seen as interfering. How can we understand their situation, and what right have we to involve ourselves unless asked? Many people are reluctant to talk publicly about their finances, their debts, or how much they earn, nor are they particularly eager to accept advice from others. Most of us are reluctant to pry, seeing it as none of our business, even though we might be very interested in the answers!

Yet there are other people who certainly like to talk and boast about their finances, albeit often in a rather indirect manner. We can think here of the proverbial dinner party conversation on house values and how lucky one particular guest has been to buy just before prices started rising (meaning, of course, how astute they were). Some people may enjoy talking about their new car or kitchen or extension precisely because of the financial consequences that can be deduced from this. In response, we will be polite and make some inconsequential reply, and perhaps ask questions that encourage them to talk about it some more (this being what they want to do anyway). We may not really be interested, but we know we cannot insult them or call them stupid for wasting their money. We may comment to our partner about what a waste it is to get a new car every two years or to buy a house that is far too big for their needs, but we would not say this to them. We appreciate that what they are doing is their own business and up to them. It is legal and legitimate and harms no one. After all, it is their money they are spending. And of course we expect the same latitude and reticence to be accorded to us, even as we might do things very differently from them.

Quite often housing finance enters our decision-making processes only part way through and not at the very beginning. We decide we want X and only then do we ask ourselves, 'Can we afford to do X?' We decide first what we want and then whether we can afford it, whether it is possible, or should we do something else? We might then weigh up what we might gain and lose. We might do some sort of informal cost-benefit analysis of the various options that present themselves. We weigh up our options and determine whether it is money well spent. But we start from the desire or aspiration and not from the money. Of course, if we have little or no income, this may well override any aspiration we might have, although this was not the case with G, who still placed her aspirations above finance. In most cases the financial decision is subservient to the aspiration. We still need the money to attain the aspiration, but the money itself is the means.

Indeed, if a dwelling is a means to an end (Clapham 2005; King 1996), then the means of paying for it is even more subsidiary: housing finance is the means to achieve a further means. Perhaps many of our transactions are like this: they help us along the path rather than getting us to the end. This shows that housing finance is actually about maintenance and continuity. If we take the path of many post-war UK households described above, we might have extended ourselves somewhat in the early years of our mortgage and this may be a struggle for us (some households who did this in the mid-2000s may lose out altogether as they find their dwelling is now worth less than their mortgage debt). But this does not mean that we have acted in this manner just for financial reasons. Spending the money is just a necessary part of living there in that dwelling. If we want to do things, we must expect to pay for them: this does not mean that paying for them is all that matters. What we want is the end, not the process.

This being so, how important to us is the fact that housing is a store of wealth? Clearly this can be very important, in that it may motivate us and some markets are almost entirely dependent on this factor, particularly the buy-to-let market. But for those of us who might be called 'normal' owner occupiers, do we really see the dwelling in terms of how much it is worth? Does this mean that we use it only in a certain manner, or change and improve it only in such a way as to increase its value? Some might answer that this is exactly what they do, but it would be interesting to see how they actually use their dwelling. Do they use it very differently from those who express no great concern about the value of their dwelling?

But, more fundamentally, what does it mean to use a dwelling – the place of security, protected intimacy, privacy – just to maximise its asset value? Have they deliberately bought something to live in primarily as an investment, as a means of relatively short-term profit? Once they are in the dwelling, what do they do? Do they still consider it their home and use it any differently than if it were the ideal? Are they less attached to it, seeing it just as a temporary means to a financial end, even as they treat the dwelling very gently so as not to damage it and thus reduce its value or increase their costs?

And how do we feel about these people? Do we consider them deluded, mercenary or sensible investors? This depends on our view of the activity of dwelling and the particular aims and expectations we might have of our own dwelling. Of course investing in property is entirely legitimate and, in a sense, is entirely necessary to maintain a stock of high-quality dwellings. But is it different when you are actually living in the 'investment' and bringing up your children there?

Of course, on one level, we can just use the dwelling as an investment. It is our home and it will still keep us warm and dry, secure and protected; it will still allow us to be intimate. Seeing the dwelling in purely financial terms does not make it any less efficient as a functioning object.

Most commonly we imagine the people who see their dwelling principally as a stepping stone to something better are young and upwardly mobile and who want to work in expensive cities like London. They might have bought a place that is far from ideal in terms of location and type, but they hope and expect it will appreciate in value, which will then allow them to purchase something better as their income grows or they marry or live with a partner. If this is the case, they are not then just buying a property as an investment, or the investment is not merely an end in itself. They are not really doing it just to make money from their dwelling. Rather they wish to live in a particular city because this is where the jobs are or where the culture is. They wish to live in London rather than elsewhere. Perhaps they feel they have to live in London. So we are again with the dichotomy of means and ends. It is still about getting a foot on the ladder; however some ladders are steeper and longer and sometimes the bottom step is a long way off the ground. This is essentially a problem for the households themselves, as we discussed earlier in the chapter, but we should accept that they have a right to do it.

People who choose to live in expensive areas take a particular subjective view of housing. We might say, as with the case of S discussed above, that they place a higher value on non-housing aspects of their life higher than on housing. But markets themselves are entities which depend upon subjective judgements about the value we place on housing and other things. This has been shown with great clarity by Thomas Sowell (2007). He states that if a house is sold for £200,000 either side of the transaction must view the value of the house differently. The buyer must view the house as being worth more than the £200,000 they have parted with. However, the seller must view the house as worth less than the £200,000 they take in place of the dwelling. If buyer and seller have precisely the same valuation, they will not agree on a sale. They must view the value of the dwelling differently. The same applies to all goods and services.

In any case market valuations are not static and depend on our expectations. We might believe that our dwelling is worth more than the market values it, and so find we cannot sell it. We then either have to alter our expectations or take the dwelling off the market. As market conditions alter, as they have done since 2006, sellers have to respond to meet the changed expectations of buyers, who feel they can offer a lower price. Prior to 2006 the situation was the reverse, with sellers in the more powerful position and better able to meet their expectations. These changes are based on nothing more than subjective values and expectations of the behaviour of others relative to our own aspirations. It is about making the most of what we have got on the basis of our understanding of what the 'most' is. This is always competitive, in that we are dealing with others with their own intentions and expectations. This means there is risk and uncertainty, but we try to engineer certainty through managing our expectations. What allows us to do this – or to attempt it – is the fact that we have choices. In most cases, we can choose when to enter a market or when to withdraw. We can, in most cases, decide to sell now or sell later. We can decide to buy a particular dwelling now, or wait in the hope that we will get a better deal on something else later on.

Of course this in itself involves a mixture of aspiration and expectations and it means playing with our time horizons, if we are so able. What matters is the importance that we place on immediate gratification or whether we are prepared to defer it, and how our expectations of markets and the behaviour of others matches up with our aspirations and our ability to manage this disjuncture. We need to judge just how necessary it is to take any action now, or whether we can put it off if the purchase doesn't seem propitious at this particular time. Are we forced to act or can we choose at our leisure?

We might suggest that we need to undertake what might be called expectations management. We need to understand our expectations and keep them in place. Indeed, without being too obtuse, we might suggest that we need to have expectations of our expectations, namely, we need to be aware of what is possible and what is achievable with regard to our plans and the ends which we have set ourselves.

I suggest that there are two types of expectations, and we need to be aware of the distinction between them. First, there are what might be called practical expectations. These are expectations that we have a realistic possibility of achieving, which relate to those choices we are able to make using resources that we have within hand. This can include money that we are able to borrow sustainably. Practical expectations are about the next step we can take with a real hope of success, and they help to inform us of whether our aspirations are in any way tenable. Second, we can define aspirational expectations, which are those that we hope to achieve but which may be long-term and only achievable as part of a staged process involving a number of steps. They may ultimately prove to be unattainable.

We can see practical expectations as the stepping stones leading to the fulfilment of our aspirational expectations. As we can seldom attain our aspirations in one step, we need to form a strategy involving staged achievements. We might defer achievement of our aspirational expectations without giving up on them. This might be what households in London are doing when they choose to buy or rent a dwelling in expectation of getting something better. Their current housing is not what they ultimately hope for, but they are doing all that is currently achievable. Their current dwelling is a staging post on the way to achieving their more long-term aspirations. Whilst they have to defer their aspirations at present, they still expect the opportunity to present itself in due time and are still working towards the fulfilment of their aspirations.

We might argue that practical expectations depend upon the past and our personal experiences, whilst aspirational expectations need not do so. We can aspire without recourse to the past. Practical expectations depend on where we are and, to an extent, on how we got there, whilst the aspirational expectations depend almost entirely on where we want to be. Problems might arise for us when there is no, or insufficient, connection between the two. We saw this in the case of G who had very high aspirational expectations, but no money. Accordingly, there was a huge gap between reality and possibility on the one hand, and fantasy and aspiration on the other. Her problems arose out of her inability to locate herself with any accuracy, and the consequent bitterness when her illusions were periodically disabused. From time to time she just could not avoid the huge disjuncture between her present and the future which she saw for herself. Her life was an attempt to keep this realisation at bay for as much of the time as possible, and we can suppose that her attitude towards money – and the lack of responsibility involved in this – was the main means by which she could do this. At certain times, when she had the money, she could at least act in the manner she thought suited her. This perhaps gave her a sense of freedom and heightened self-esteem, even if it was short-lived and followed by the inevitable low after the money had gone.

We might usefully here return to John Turner (1976) and his work on the attempts of households in Latin America to provide housing for themselves. Turner wanted to show that government intervention is not always helpful and that instead households and communities are often better able to provide for themselves if they are just given the right resources and the space in which to use them. In his book *Housing by People* (1976) he articulates two case studies carried out in Mexico City in 1971. He compares the provisional shack of a young rag-picker and his family with that of a modern government-subsidised dwelling lived in by a semi-employed middle-aged mason and his family.

The dwelling of the rag-picker and his family is literally a shack of corrugated iron and wood located in the rear yard of a family member's house. It has very basic amenities yet, Turner argues, it is supportive. It is near to the family's source of income, close to family and friends, and cheap enough to allow them to survive, with the hope of obtaining a better dwelling as their prospects improve. It thus offers them considerable freedom, and Turner thus refers to it as the 'supportive shack' (1976: 54). It is very basic accommodation, yet it fulfils the family's immediate needs and allows them to control their environment.

By contrast to that of the rag-picker, the dwelling of the mason's family is a modern house in a purpose-built estate paid for by government subsidy. However, it is located away from the family's network of friends and, crucially, away from the mason's place of employment. The mason pays out 5 per cent of his income in transport costs to and from work, in addition to the 55 per cent spent on rent and utility charges. Moreover, his wife had run a small vending business from their previous dwelling, which was forbidden under the tenancy regulations. Thus their income had reduced as their housing and transport costs had risen. Turner refers to this case as the 'oppressive house' (1976: 56). So an improvement in material standards can be counterproductive because, being based on an abstraction, material standards cannot take into account the particular needs and conditions of the household. Turner therefore concludes from these cases that material standards are not necessarily the most useful measure. He states, 'Some of the poorest dwellings, materially speaking, were clearly the best, socially speaking, and some, but not all of the highest standard dwellings, were the most socially aggressive' (1976: 52).

Turner argues that the use of government subsidies does not necessarily lead to a material improvement in the lives of people. For him, the problem is the wrong set of values imposed by government. These values are economic and based on material standards. Turner instead argues for what he calls human values, which emphasise the use to which they can be put and the level of control that the household can exercise over their immediate environment (King 1996). This necessitates access to resources, but these should be on the terms of the household and the local community rather than those of central government.

We shall consider in some detail the role of government in the next three chapters, but the importance of Turner's work for our discussion on expectations is to show how the specific circumstances of the individual household are much more important than the level of amenity in determining long-term sustainability. The issue is that people are much more capable in determining their own interests and managing their expectations than government is often prepared to admit.

Turner's discussion brings us back to the issue of choice. The rag-picker's family appears to have fewer options open to them, but Turner seems to suggest that over the long term they have more choices and that their aspirational expectations might be more attainable. They are better able to plot a course to achieve their aspirations than the mason's family who are heavily constrained by their housing.

We might consider just how much choice we do have and what this depends on. Clearly, the level of choice differs between households. It is perhaps inevitable that some people will have more choice than others, and this will be due to any number of circumstances, such as their income, their place in the lifecycle and their current housing. In terms of linking choices to expectations we have to question whether we have a really accurate sense of what our choices are. In particular, do we believe we have more or less choice than we actually have? Some people might believe that they have more options open to them than actually exist, and so act recklessly. Perhaps more likely, however, is for people to believe that they have less choice than they actually do. This might be because of natural caution, lack of knowledge, or the effect of habit and ordinary routine, which results in people operating only in certain ways rather than rationally searching out all opportunities. But it is also because their aspirations might limit them to a narrower range of options than are actually open to them. Some people, for instance, might not consider living in certain areas of a city or in certain types of property.

People who believe they have more choices than actually exist – the case of G again – risk harm, in that they might fail to appreciate the full range of consequences that may result from their decision-making. When we have no choice, it is not that we cannot make decisions, rather that we should not. We can spend on a credit card or take out a loan or extend our mortgage, but we should not have done these things, and if we were properly aware of our actual position, then we would not have done them.

Does this mean that some people should not be encouraged or even allowed to choose? Should they be prevented from taking decisions that might harm them, or should they be allowed to act so long as they do not harm anyone other than themselves? This is the classical position detailed by John Stuart Mill ([1859] 1974) on the limits of individual freedom: that the only limit in a civilised society is to prevent harm to others, but that, as a consequence, we allow individuals to act as they please even if they harm themselves. The problems with this position are well known. First, can we be sure that we have isolated the effects of any one act so that it will not impact on others? And, second, should we really sit back and take no action when we know that an individual might – or probably will – choose badly? If we have a justifiable reason to believe that someone cannot act properly and so will harm themselves, is it acceptable still to leave them to get on with it? In response, a libertarian like Charles Murray (1984) might argue that we cannot be so fine-grained in our interventions to ensure that we limit our assistance only to those we definitely know will – or do – need our help. If we seek to pre-empt actions, we tend to hamper the choices of many who are capable. We might even argue that this constraint is legitimate if it prevents suffering, even if we do not know exactly who is affected. Yet this is an argument that we cannot properly substantiate and can be used to justify blanket interventions for the 'good' of society as a whole.

## A desire to own

We might say that we live in societies that legitimate aspiration. Western societies have become increasingly choice-based and so seek to expand the possibility of fulfilling expectations. This, we might argue, is the principal virtue of a free society, which encourages individuals to achieve their ends through markets. In countries like the US and the UK one way this is manifested is through owner occupation. In both countries this is the dominant tenure with around 70 per cent of households in the sector.

People become owner-occupiers because they want to and because they can. Indeed they now expect it. It is this expectation, and the practical possibility of its achievement, that determines behaviour. Owning houses, for good or ill, is simply what most households seek to do and, by and large, they are able to attain and sustain this. It is this aspirational expectation that creates the desire to own, which in turn drives much of housing policy in the UK and US. We need to understand and come to terms with this desire, because it is this that creates housing booms and busts. We might even suggest, as perverse as it may sound, that one of the reasons for the depth of the recession in housing markets since 2007 is precisely because individuals are correct in their desire to own. They are all too aware that it is in their best interests to pursue owner occupation. They believe owning to be superior to renting in most cases. This is not natural: other countries do things differently and their financial crises have also manifested themselves differently, if no less dramatically (e.g. the loss of export markets in the case of both China and Germany). But in the Anglo-Saxon world, ownership is crucial: it is what people consider that they must have. Ownership is now so embedded in the culture of the US and UK that there are no real alternatives. The dominance of owner occupation becomes self-fulfilling and self-justifying.

This, however, has a number of consequences. First, because owner occupation is such a dominant tenure it acts, as it were, as a funnel for aspirational expectations. Our expectations become focused upon this one objective. This means that the manner in which housing markets operate can have a considerable influence over the well-being of households and their ability to fulfil their aspirations.

Second, the scale of owner occupation means that there are no real incentives in the UK and US to shift away from owner occupation. It is difficult, if not impossible, to envisage a situation in which any other tenure can compete with owner occupation. Therefore what matters now is not the size of the tenure itself, or indeed whether we desire to own and whether this can change, but rather the stability of housing markets as the main means of fulfilment for the majority of households. In pragmatic terms, the debate has shifted away from whether we should or should not own to how markets enable individual households to buy and sell housing when they wish to.

Third, the fact that there are no longer any alternatives to owner occupation and that the desire to own is taken for granted means that the recession of 2008 is different from all previous recessions. Owner occupation is now so dominant that any decline in housing markets will have a much more general effect.

## Conclusions

In this chapter I have meandered through a number of speculations on expectations and how they affect the way we face markets. My aim has been to demonstrate that it is subjective behaviour, based on aspirational expectations, which determines how we use markets and how seriously we take housing finance. We use our own resources, what I have termed really private finance, to fulfil our ends, and this separates us from any particular institutional framework. This means that we must bear the responsibility for our actions.

This is the context in which we should consider boom and bust in housing markets. We tend to view markets as abstractions, as things that are 'out there', whilst we just get on with our lives using the resources that are available to us. One of the key resources we use is our dwelling itself. This separation we have between ourselves and markets helps us to understand the relationship we have with our housing, as an object we use and which thus becomes meaningful. But it also means that we relate to markets in a rather oblique way. We engage with markets not because of any intrinsic qualities of market activity, but rather to achieve our ends. Markets can work very well in helping us, but we are also capable of misunderstanding them and engaging with them without a realistic set of expectations.

Finally, this discussion will have made it clear that when we talk of housing boom and bust, what we are really discussing is a number of personal tragedies. This is a situation in which individual households have found they cannot fulfil their aspirations. Indeed the households themselves might be torn apart and the relationship with their dwelling ended. The financial crisis is destructive at the individual level, and we need to place this at the very centre of our discussions. We might tend to focus on the mistakes made by banks and other institutions; we can quite properly pick on the failures of regulators and policy-makers; we can argue about the merits of globalisation and Anglo-Saxon capitalism. But all the time we should hold in our minds that this is a series of personal tragedies, each with its own history, its own causality and its own dramatic ending. We should look at housing boom and bust with our consciences well and truly pricked.

# Chapter 3

# Lots of bad decisions

## Introduction

Our life course is determined by a series of decisions that we make. Some we make because we have to, others because we want to. Some of these decisions matter more than others. We might choose to marry or live with a partner: in other words, we form a household with at least one other. This involves making a choice, but also somebody else choosing us. Once we have chosen we expect, or we hope, that this relationship is permanent and we act accordingly. We make joint plans, and one of the most important is about where we live. We choose where we wish to live and how much we are prepared to spend. We need to decide this on the basis of what is available in the place where we want to live and how our priority for housing compares with other areas of expenditure. Is our housing the priority, or do we place a higher premium on other activities? Do we wish to forgo some activities – entertaining, going out, holidays – so we can afford our dream home now? Is our priority immediate consumption, or do we start to save for when we are older and need looking after, or for when we have a family?

We can choose whether we have a family or not, or rather we can make plans and work to put them into effect. We might be fortunate and have children when we want and in the numbers desired, but then we might not and so become frustrated. However, we might decide that we do not wish to have any children, at least not for the present. But once we have children, we find our ability to choose, our freedom to act on the spur of the moment and just for ourselves, heavily circumscribed. We find that the demands of our children are unconditional and they limit our mobility and our income. In any case, we need to make decisions about our work. How ambitious are we? Are we prepared to work anywhere, and what does our partner think about this? Do we put our work above all else and so perhaps put off starting a family? Or do we put the children first and so one partner gives up work, if we can afford to do this or are prepared to make the necessary sacrifices?

It is obvious that these choices are all interconnected, and one decision we make can affect another. We can close off one possibility by the choices made to deal with another issue. Choosing to spend all our income now has consequences for the future when we are thinking of retirement. The problem is that many of the choices we make are not reversible, even though the consequences of some might not be clear for many years. All of our choices are consequential. Of course the consequences will differ, from the minor to the significant. However, we may not be able to spot their significance before it really starts to matter.

All of these decisions are about relationships, some of which are formal and some are informal. There are differences in these relations, in that some are more directly controllable than others. We can choose partners – we have an absolute veto, so to speak, but then so do they. We can plan not to have children with some certainty, even if it means abstinence, but planning for them is not so certain and, once we have children we find ourselves constrained in particular ways and are forced to make other decisions. We can choose to work in a certain profession or job, but we have to find such a job and keep it. We might decide to live in a certain area or a particular type of dwelling. We can choose a house, but it has to be for sale and we have to be able to afford it. We can move when we please, but we have to have somewhere to go and we may be constrained by our children and our partner. We can decide how much we save, but we cannot set the conditions for this in terms of interest rates, the deals on offer or issues such as inflation, which might affect our ability to save.

In many cases we are at the mercy of forces that are much larger than ourselves. We cannot determine inflation or the state of housing and labour markets. We are connected to global networks, as part of a large interconnected structure, in which decisions have consequences – for ourselves and others – and in which some decisions, taken at key nodal points in the network, can be extremely consequential for us and all others, yet we are not party to many of these decisions.

This does not detract from the fact that these decisions relate to issues that are often extremely personal. Decisions about moving house, changing jobs, having children and where we put our savings are decisions we tend to take at most with one other, and that person has to be special and close to us. However, our ability to make choices, and to control the outcomes, can be determined by matters so very far away from us and very much out of our control. We can make choices and we can be aware, in general terms, that these have consequences, yet we cannot be aware of how we might be affected or when.

Of course we might not be personally affected that much or even at all. Unemployment has increased in the US and UK since 2008, but most people are still in work, with employment rates still over 90 per cent in mid-2009. Likewise, house repossessions have increased, but again these represent only a very tiny percentage of the total number of mortgages. Pension funds, too, have fallen in value, but not down to zero. This means that some of us will be affected but others will not.

However, for those who have been affected, the consequences can be total. We go from having a job to not having one; from having a home to not; from having savings and a secure future to being penniless. These are personal tragedies and we may find it hard to cope with them, or to recover even after a long period of time. We might find another job, or be able to rent a decent dwelling that we can afford, and our savings might recover, but then we might not. We might not see any way out of this catastrophe that has befallen us, and we feel it might have happened despite our best efforts to take care of ourselves and our family. We might believe, entirely legitimately, that it is not our fault.

There is a balance that needs to be struck here. When we use the phrase 'boom and bust' we risk becoming too general. Boom and bust implies an ongoing cycle, in which house prices go up and then inevitably come back down again, before the cycle starts all over again. It is all too easy to see this as an abstraction, as an economic phenomenon with its own existence. What we do is to aggregate all the millions of consequences and reify this into 'the problem' or 'the crisis'. There is a danger, therefore, that we see boom and bust as an anonymous and empty cycle of events, which can be dealt with by technical solutions at the macro level. Boom and bust becomes, as it were, just one thing rather than millions of events that are interconnected, but where each is total in its consequences. Boom and bust, or the millions of events that this has become the shorthand for, is consequential primarily at the level of individuals in their roles as members of a household, as employees, as savers, and so on.

Here we are not considering just one thing: it is about people making choices based on their needs, wants, aspirations and expectations. They form households, have children, buy and sell houses, work and save (or do not) – all based on constrained choice. It is a story about increasing affluence and of aspirations being fulfilled. But it is also a story of failure, on the part of some, to meet or sustain their aspirations and expectations. The story, so to speak, has something of a plot twist. People now realise that they were wrong not to have saved more or spent less; that they were wrong to have used a particular type of mortgage to buy a house that, in hindsight, they really couldn't afford; that they were wrong to assume their job was safe and to have spent accordingly; that they were wrong to believe that their house would continue to rise in value.

Does this mean that these people were stupid? How could they have been so wrong about so many things? And does the fact that they were in good company make any difference? After all, not many people could honestly claim to see the bust coming, and no one was able to prevent it. We could suggest that politicians and bankers took advantage of the gullibility of these households by offering them something that was not sustainable in return for votes and profits. In a sense, of course, they did. Politicians certainly played on the aspirations that many had to own their own home and lead a more affluent existence. Bankers were more than happy to play along and offer the rope with which people could later hang themselves. But then, isn't this precisely what we would expect politicians and bankers to do? Politicians seek to remain popular and in office and bankers seek a good rate of return.

We shall consider these issues in more detail in Chapter 4, when we try to explain what happened. But, for now, we might respond to the claims of gullibility by suggesting that what actually occurred was quite rational in the circumstances. Households took decisions that appeared rational on the basis of the information available to them at the time. They had no reason to believe they were wrong at the time, and this means they were acting rationally, even if, in hindsight, it was mistaken.

However, we make choices in situations in which we do not have complete control, and in which we cannot determine the outcome of the story. This is not because of our ignorance, stupidity or anyone's bad faith, but simply because we operate within complex open systems where our personal control is quite minimal, even though we might feel, for most of the time, to be in control of what is going on around us. We feel we can choose because we have done so in the past. We feel in control and that we can use what is around us to insulate and support us. Indeed, the fact that we tend to focus on our own aspirations and choices, and that these enclose us, helps us to forget the wider consequences that can ensue when our actions mix with those of many others.

This is the context in which we should view any discussion of the events in housing markets since 2006. We have to see it in these terms: individuals are generally competent, but not omni-competent; they control many things, but not all things; they act on the basis of what they believe to be the case, even though they do not have complete information. Most of us, most of the time, are making the best of what we have in the conditions that pertain at the time.

In this chapter we consider the nature of what has befallen households in the 2000s. It is necessarily an incomplete picture because the situation is both extremely complex and is still unfolding. We shall make some attempt to discuss the wider impact of the financial crisis, but our focus will remain primarily on housing and will touch on the wider issues only when it is necessary for a fuller explanation. Indeed this chapter will focus on explanation, whilst Chapter 4 concentrates more on how it has come about and why. One further problem is how to build a consistent and coherent narrative in which everything seems to fit together. It is therefore difficult to know exactly where to start and what to put first. Clearly, there is a distinctly UK dimension and also an American one, and there are many important differences. However, I have tried to draw out areas of commonality. This, as we shall see in Chapter 4, has implications for the political causes and consequences of housing boom and bust.

Up to this point the discussion has focused on the decisions and aspirations of individuals. This has been a deliberate tactic to locate the nature of the crisis in the personal. The discussion now inevitably takes a turn towards the more general by looking at the manner in which the last boom and bust occurred and how this happened. However, these events have been well and truly contextualised to show that, whilst they may be global in their scope and scale, their implications are all too local. Politics, we might suggest, concerns the ability to appreciate the aspirations and expectations of people and to seek to meet them, moderate them or even to try to control and alter them. So what follows is the story of how the expectations and aspirations of very many people have been so determined.

## Government encouragement

Governments in both the UK and US have supported owner occupation over many years, and they have done so because of the tenure's virtues of inculcating independence and personal responsibility. The tenure has been one of the main ways in which successive governments have promoted the 'property-owning democracy'. This particular phrase is, of course, now somewhat hackneyed and has lost much of its freshness and appeal. This is partly because of its association with the politics of the 1980s: for example, policies such as the Right to Buy and the privatisation of public utilities in the UK. Yet we should not forget that for much of the twentieth century the appeal of this ideal was very strong. Owner occupation as a tenure has retained a basic popularity across nearly all social classes, and governments have long seen the need to encourage this desire.

Ferguson (2008) suggests that the promotion of the ideal of the property-owning democracy really began in post-depression America. He characterises the tenure at this period as being based on short-term (three to five years) interest-only mortgages, which meant that the mortgagee faced a very large final payment or the need to remortgage at regular intervals. The depression after 1929 had a disastrous impact on this market, with a precipitous fall in land values and massive increases in unemployment. As a result many households lost their dwellings.

In response to this the Hoover and Roosevelt administrations chose to intervene to create a more stable mortgage market. This was achieved by allowing for the development of long-term mortgage finance and by underpinning the market through a system of deposit insurance. The Roosevelt administration created the Federal Housing Administration which provided federal insurance for mortgage lenders and encouraged long-term (20-year), fully amortised, low-interest loans. In effect this provided a form of nationwide standardisation and regulation of the mortgage market in the US. Further impetus was given by the creation of the Federal National Mortgage Association – known as Fannie Mae – with the role of issuing bonds and using the proceeds to buy mortgages from local Savings and Loans.[1] In return, the Savings and Loans were restricted to providing finance to depositors at low rates. The result of this institutional backing was a mortgage market based on fixed long-term interest rates and security of deposits. Accordingly, it is no exaggeration to state, as Ferguson does, that 'the US government was effectively underwriting the mortgage market, encouraging lenders and borrowers to get together' (2008: 249).

---

1 The equivalent of UK building societies.

The situation in the UK was similar, if less clear cut in terms of government intervention, but the increase in owner occupation was still significant. As with the US, the inter-war period saw an increase in owner occupation in the UK. The 1930s was a period of rising real incomes, but static house prices, and it saw the development of building societies as sources of secure and stable investment which maintained a high degree of liquidity. The result was a boom in owner occupation fuelled by competition amongst building societies flush with funds. Thus the fastest-growing sector in the inter-war years was owner occupation, and this boom in owner occupation in the 1930s occurred during a period when subsidies to local authorities were being substantially cut (Boddy 1992). The growth of owner occupation was further encouraged by the improvement in transport links, particularly around London and other major cities, allowing for suburbanisation and the popularity of the semi-detached house.

In the UK the period after the Second World War is closely associated with the development of council housing, and indeed the effect of continued rationing into the early 1950s did mean a reduction in the building of owner-occupied housing. However, the increasing affluence of the later 1950s and 1960s saw a renewed growth in owner occupation, such that by the 1971 Census over half of households were owner occupiers (Malpass and Murie 1999). As was the case in the US, owning one's own dwelling was now becoming the norm rather than the exception, and increasingly it was becoming the expectation of the majority.

The election of the Conservatives under Mrs Thatcher in 1979 gave this move towards owner occupation a renewed push, particularly through the introduction of the Right to Buy (RTB) in 1981. This policy allowed the sitting tenants of local authority housing to purchase their dwelling at discounts of up to 60 per cent. Applicants had not just the right to purchase their existing dwelling, but also had the right to a 100 per cent mortgage from the local authority at a rate of interest fixed by the Treasury. In total, 2.5 million dwellings were sold under the RTB, and this was one of the main reasons for the increase in owner occupation to 70 per cent by the end of the century (King 2010). This means that owner occupation in the UK is now at a slightly higher level than in the US.

But the RTB is important for a further reason, and this has a particular importance for our story of housing boom and bust. Prior to the RTB, access to owner occupation depended on a household's ability to save for a deposit and obtain a mortgage from a building society. Often this necessitated long-term saving, as well as a regular income. So, whilst owner occupation had been extended beyond the affluent, there were still many households whose aspirations to own their own dwelling went unfulfilled. The RTB went some way towards dealing with this, as did the liberalisation of the mortgage market in the 1980s, which allowed banks to enter the mortgage market and removed many of the restrictions on lending. The result was an increase in competition and an opening up of the market to the benefit of many households hitherto unable to access owner occupation. This was further supported by tax relief on mortgage interest and the abolition of imputed rental income tax[2] in 1962. By 1991 this subsidy was enjoyed by 9.6 million households at a cost to the Treasury of £7.7 billion.

The importance of these developments in the 1980s and beyond was that government was now actively encouraging and supporting working-class households into owner occupation, and found that these households were only too keen to take up the offer. We can see some similarities to this in the US, with attempts from the 1970s onwards to encourage lower-income groups into owner occupation. As Ferguson (2008) shows, this had a racial dimension, in that black households were largely excluded from the booms in owning both before and after the Second World War. Certain areas of American cities were 'redlined', effectively denying access to mortgage finance to households in poorer areas of low-quality housing with higher levels of benefit dependency and unemployment (Butler 2009). Black and Hispanic households were over-represented in these redlined areas and so found themselves outside the

---

2 This was a tax levied on the assumed rental income an owner would receive from renting from themselves.

property-owning democracy. The Carter administration sought to attend to this problem in two ways: first, the Home Mortgage Disclosure Act 1975 forced lenders to provide information on who they lent to; second, the Community Reinvestment Act 1977 made the practice of redlining illegal. Lenders could not favour suburban districts over inner city areas and had to serve their geographical area equally well. The 1977 Act has been amended over time, with a particularly important change introduced by the Clinton administration in 1995 which allowed – Butler suggests 'forced' (2009: 53) – lenders to ignore the usual tests of creditworthiness in making loan decisions. The pressure on lenders was now to open up access to all parts of the community, regardless of credit history or indeed even their ability to fund such a long-term commitment.

The rhetoric underpinning this support for owner occupation became more grandiose over time, and the effect was to shift the manner in which owner occupation was viewed away from what might be seen as a privilege – as something dependent on having the income required to sustain the tenure, as well as behaving in a responsible manner – to that of a right. President Bush stated in 2002 that he wanted every American to own their own home (Ferguson 2008), and signed the wonderfully titled American Dream Downpayment Act into law in 2003. This Act sought to create an additional 5.5 million new minority owner occupiers by 2010. Lenders were pressured not to seek full documentation and Fannie Mae and Freddie Mac[3] were encouraged to under-write sub-prime loans for the first time.

In the UK the Blair government also sought to extend owner occupation to those on low incomes. A five-year plan entitled Homes for All was announced in early 2005, and introduced several measures aimed at assisting households into owner occupation. These included a First Time Buyers Initiative, which allowed low-income households and key workers to buy an equity share in their dwelling, and an initiative called HomeBuy

---

3 This is the Federal Home Loan Mortgage Corporation, established in 1970 to provide competition to Fannie Mae in the secondary mortgage market when the latter was privatised.

for social housing tenants to enable them to buy, at a discount, an equity share in their dwelling of between 50 and 100 per cent (King 2006). The HomeBuy policy has been developed subsequently and extended to include non-tenants.

The Homes for All agenda differs from past attempts to encourage owner occupation in that the justification for it was not so much that of independence, or even choice, as was the case with the RTB, but social justice. The government's argument was that low-income households deserved access to owner occupation as much as the more affluent ones that already had ready access. Traditionally, of course, social housing has been justified on the basis of social justice (Brown 1999), but now the concept has been extended to include ownership. Indeed, the approach of the Blair government was to divert resources away from social housing and towards owner occupation, and to do so in the name of social justice.

This discussion shows that governments, in both the UK and US, have sought to encourage owner occupation. They have done this on the grounds that the tenure is popular and is what the majority aspire to. However, as owner occupation has become so dominant and seen as the normal tenure, government has extended its support to all parts of society rather than limiting its support to a general level based on maintaining stability and fair dealing. The effect of this, we might suggest, has been the very opposite: instead of stability we have seen increasing instability as more and more marginal households quite naturally take up the offer of owner occupation presented to them by government. This intervention, we can now see, has sown the seeds of the problems of boom and bust. But this is not yet a complete picture. We have dealt with the issue of government intervention, but we should also be aware that the pursuit of property ownership – its glorification even – has become one of the great cultural phenomena of our times.

## The new porn?

Here I do not want to suggest any form of determinism or to give the impression that individual households have been led into owner occupation by government. No one is forced to buy a dwelling, and we must presume that all those who bought have done so because it was what they expressly wanted. Many may have fallen into it, as it were, naturally: it is simply what you do; their parents being owner occupiers, so they have done likewise. Others have taken the opportunities provided by government but might not have done so quite as readily without this support. However, they were not compelled to do so, and this is an important factor to remember. As we stated at the start of this chapter, households choose to become owner-occupiers. They do so because they desire it and because they feel they can achieve it. We might say that government is as much responding to this desire as leading or creating it.

Indeed this desire is important in feeding the growth of owner occupation. Over the last two decades households in the UK and the US have become obsessed by property to the extent that it is glorified and objectified in an almost pornographic way. TV channels seem to be full of programmes on purchasing properties or on doing them up. Many of us sit transfixed as others go through the apparent agonies of deciding on the right property, whether they can afford it and then how to redesign it. Such programmes have made the careers of so-called experts, who are able to advise on design or lead naive couples through the complexities of house buying. Indeed one of these supposed experts was appointed by David Cameron, the leader of the Conservative Party, to be his housing adviser. These programmes, with their telegenic experts, offered the prospect that households could surf the housing boom, spot a bargain and improve it in a manner that would enhance its value (with the implication it could be sold on at a profit).

This fetishisation of property is considered by Garber (2000) in a book titled *Sex and Real Estate*. She considers that the concern for houses and their interiors has replaced sex as the main preoccupation of many households. This is because she sees the same sense of desire for property and furnishing as for the bodies of those we love and desire. The subtitle of the book is *Why We Love Houses* and she indulges in some loving descriptions of kitchen worktops and soft furnishing. Garber suggests that we have affairs with our dwellings, falling in love with them and carrying on the affair with great intensity, before having our eyes turned by something else that comes along. She is somewhat ambivalent about this herself: on the one hand, she is an academic and able to look at the phenomenon with a degree of detachment; on the other hand, she admits to being sucked into this circuit of desire, so that much of the material for her book is from her own experience.

Garber's attitude is rather typical of the ambivalence we see with regard to property: it has an immense symbolic significance, whilst at the same time being a place that fulfils an existential need. Nowhere is this ambivalence more evident than in the generic name given to domestic design magazines in the US. As Garber reports, they are referred to as shelter magazines, a designation which carries with it the notion of an imperative condition that could not be further from the concerns of these magazines, with their emphasis on contemporary design and articles on luxury dwellings owned by the rich and famous. Indeed for many people in the UK the term 'shelter' is now so closely associated with the most high-profile homeless charity as to make the use of the term in the US seem almost offensive. What could be more inappropriate than the peddling of luxury on an existential condition?

One aspect then of this glorification of property is that we lose sight of what it is for. We might forget that it is a place to live in, to raise a family, to be intimate and close to those we love. The dwelling becomes more than a place, but takes the form of an object of desire. What we have, when we link this to the support to owner occupation given by government, is a potentially toxic mix in which property is something we obsessively desire, but which is then promoted by government and subsidised precisely because it is so desired. Government sees an imperative to help us make the down payment on our dream. It is after all one we all share and why should anyone be left out? But this support only legitimises our desire, and this makes it easier for us to choose. But, perhaps in doing so, we start to forget the consequences that often go with choosing.

## The end of boom and bust?

So the priority of housing policy in the UK and US has increasingly been about extending owner occupation, and this has been at a time of a growing popular obsession with property. But there has been a further factor that is very important in understanding what occurred after 2006. Since 1993 most of the developed world has seen a period of almost continuous economic growth. In the UK after the humiliation of being forced to leave the Exchange Rate Mechanism in 1992, the Major and Blair governments operated within increasingly benign economic conditions, with growing world trade, high levels of employment and low inflation. This was the period of the 'Goldilocks economy' – not too hot, but not too cold – when government was able to chart a course for stable economic growth and increased prosperity.

The symbol of this benign period was the boast of the UK Chancellor of the Exchequer, Gordon Brown, namely, to have ended boom and bust. As a result of the apparently prudent policies introduced since 1997, Brown was able to 'guarantee' that there would be no return to the booms followed by the inevitable busts that have typified British economic history since the 1960s. One of his first acts as Chancellor was to give the Bank of England control over the setting of interest rates, and so he was able to claim there would be no direct political control over the key levers of the economy.

Politically this rhetoric was a spectacular success, with New Labour going on to win elections in 2001 and 2005, and with Brown himself becoming prime minister in 2007. It also allowed Brown to pursue a policy that was in many ways the direct opposite of that which his rhetoric proclaimed. He argued for a cautious and prudent approach so that the UK would avoid boom and bust, but in reality he undertook a quite massive increase in government expenditure and an expansion of the public sector. The government planned and undertook a programme of what it termed 'investment' in key areas of the public sector, such as health and education (but not housing, at least not to the same extent), leading to a tripling of health spending between 2001 and 2010. The government was successful in labelling the previous Conservative administrations between 1979 and 1997 as having 'underinvested' in the public services and so was able to feed on a growing sense of dissatisfaction with health and education provision in particular.

Such an increase in government spending was portrayed by government as being affordable on a long-term basis. The booming economy allowed for increasing tax revenues, even as the government maintained income tax rates at low levels. Two sources of this increased tax revenue were especially relevant to what happened after 2006. First, a significant element of the increased revenue came from the financial services sector, which grew largely as a result of Brown's deliberate policy of light-touch regulation. Bank profits became a reliable source of Corporation Tax, and the salaries and bonuses of the highly paid financial sector were also growing in importance. Second, the government came to rely increasingly on revenue from Stamp Duty on the sale of housing. As house prices and the number of sales increased, so did government revenues.

The UK government therefore was able to promote economic growth between 2000 and 2006 not as a boom, but as a sustainable pattern brought about by prudent policies. Politically it could point to increased public spending, whilst economically it could take the credit for high levels of employment and low inflation. Yet Brown's approach to the economy was very much a one-club policy, in that it depended entirely upon maintaining economic growth. This lack of any alternative approach became more apparent as New Labour turned to ever higher levels of public borrowing even as the economy continued to grow. In order to fund its programme of public spending without increasing direct taxes on households or business, the government was drawn into borrowing, always backed with optimistic promises that the borrowing was affordable – within what Brown termed his Golden Rules – and would be paid back in the near future.

This pattern of high spending and borrowing was matched by the Bush administration in the US, which turned a budget surplus of 4 per cent of GDP in 2000 to a deficit of 2.5–3 per cent in 2008 (Cable 2009). The shift in public spending might be seen as less planned and based on differing priorities, particularly relating to tax cuts and military spending on the Afghan and Iraq wars, but it did have the same effect of increasing government borrowing at a time of relative economic prosperity.

A further area of commonality between the UK and the US was the rapid increase in private and corporate debt. Not only was government debt increasing, but companies were relying more on leverage to fund expansion and acquisitions, and households were extending themselves by taking on additional debt in the form of credit cards and mortgage finance. The savings ratio in both countries declined markedly and by 2006 was actually negative in the US. The result was an increasing dependence in the UK and US on foreign borrowing, particularly from China and the Middle East (Wolf 2009). The UK and the US were becoming the consumers of Chinese savings, and so dependent on the continued preparedness of the Chinese to lend.

However, this reliance on consumption and foreign investment on the part of the UK and US economies was largely ignored by politicians and households alike. The perception was of increasing affluence as house prices increased and cheap credit remained readily available. Indeed it became a matter of policy to attempt to maintain consumption at this high level. The response of the central banks was to ensure that money remained cheap and credit readily available through loose monetary policy (Booth 2009; Congdon 2009). The Chairman of the Federal Reserve, Alan Greenspan, made a point of arguing that it was not possible to pre-empt a boom and it was much better – and less disruptive – to clear up a burst bubble than to try and prick one (Greenspan 2007; Shiller 2008). As a result there was no real attempt at monetary tightening; indeed quite the reverse as bankers and politicians alike sought to maintain the feel-good factor of increasing house values and high levels of personal consumption.

In the UK and US deliberately counter-cyclical policies aimed at meeting political objectives were being persued. The Bush administration had its wars and tax cuts and the Blair/Brown governments had their desire to improve health and education whilst keeping direct taxation low. To maintain this, both governments needed to ensure that their economies boomed and borrowing remained cheap. Therefore they needed to maintain an optimistic rhetoric that we were now in a new economic paradigm in which the old rules no longer applied (Shiller 2008). The economic conditions between 2000 and 2006 had to be portrayed as sustainable and permanent. Both Greenspan and Brown may have genuinely believed this, or it might have been a risk they thought was worth taking. However, we now know they were wrong.

## It all goes wrong

To recap, we have described a situation in which governments have sought to encourage owner occupation for all households and within a climate of the popular glorification of property. More broadly, this was taking place during a prolonged period of economic growth, which governments were regarding as permanent and demonstrative of a new economic era.

It is clear, with hindsight, that this was a mistaken view and depended on continued growth and popular confidence. What overturned this perception was the collapse of the US sub-prime mortgage market in 2006. Sub-prime mortgages were sold to households with a poor credit history and often with little in the way of existing assets. Ferguson (2008) refers to them as NINJA loans: no income, no job, no assets. As we have seen, lenders were encouraged by government to lend to low-income households, and Fannie Mae and Freddie Mac were likewise encouraged to purchase these mortgages and so give them explicit support. Indeed, the role of these institutions changed from purchasing only high-grade securities to the active encouragement of sub-prime lending.

Such mortgages were attractive to households because of their initial low rate of interest. This made the loan affordable in the short term, but there was a sting in the tail, in that the interest rate was scheduled to increase after the initial period. Perhaps households were persuaded that they could remortgage their house before the period ended and so keep on with the low rate, and this might have been possible if house prices had continued to rise in the US. However, 2006 saw falls in prices in some cities (Shiller 2008), which made remortgaging impossible and so households found themselves with higher repayments on what was now a declining asset.

This situation was compounded by the nature of the US mortgage market and particularly the fact that lenders tended to fund their lending through the sale of assets (i.e. mortgage debt) rather than through the deposits of savers, as was the case with the building societies in the UK. As we have seen, the US mortgage market grew in the 1930s as a result of the backing given by government agencies which offered securitisation to lenders. But it was this means of supporting lenders which actually allowed the sub-prime market to thrive. Lenders could pass on their risky NINJA loans to other investors in return for continued funding. These investors would be national banks, such as Lehman Brothers based in New York, who were happy to take the higher interest that came with these riskier loans. Mortgage brokers were, of course, more than happy to pass on these loans to others and continue with their lucrative trade.

In turn the banks would then sell this risk on in the form of collateralised debt obligations (CDOs). This involved the combining of sub-prime mortgages with other less risky loans and selling them on to investors. These CDOs were often given the highest rating from ratings agencies like Standard & Poor's and Fitch on the basis that they contained at least some high-quality debt. The belief was that the use of these financial products would spread the risk across financial institutions and was therefore of benefit to global financial markets. Sharing this debt around meant that the liability of any one institution would be limited.

The problem, however, was that these financial instruments were based on rather shaky foundations. This was not readily apparent whilst house prices continued to rise and sub-prime borrowers could afford their repayments. But once the sub-prime market began to collapse, it soon became evident that these debt obligations were potentially worthless and that the sharing of risk was not a means of protection, but a form of infection.

Instead of only a few local institutions being affected by mortgage default, the ripples were felt across the world.

A further complicating factor was the rapid increase in oil, commodity and food prices that was occurring at the same time as cracks were appearing in the US and UK mortgage markets. The rapid economic expansion of China and, to a lesser extent, India had increased the demand for raw materials and food and led to rapid inflation in prices (Cable 2009). Likewise, oil prices rose steadily in the mid-2000s, but increased dramatically in mid-2008 to $140 a barrel. The reasons for this spike in oil prices – the price fell dramatically at the end of 2008 – are complex and beyond the scope of this book (see Cable 2009 for an interesting discussion on the causes). However, the outcome of this was rapid inflation in 2008, leading to the policy response by central banks across the world to increase interest rates. This monetary tightening can now be seen to have been singularly ill-timed, in that it impacted on mortgage costs just at a time when confidence was dropping in the US and UK housing markets. The increase in housing costs in 2008 had the effect of heightening the sub-prime mortgage crisis, leading to a further wave of foreclosures and a downward spiral in house prices.

The mortgage market in the UK had traditionally operated differently from that of the US. Building societies typically funded their loans through the deposits of their savers and depended much less on the wholesale money markets. The result was that building societies were cautious, low-risk institutions. The downside of this, however, was that they were discouraged from innovation and tended to be small and only local in their reach.

This situation began to change with the deregulation of the market in the mid-1980s, which allowed the high-street banks to provide mortgage finance and the building societies to diversify. One effect of this was that many of the larger building societies became banks by demutualising (building societies were owned by their depositors) and became publicly traded companies. This allowed them to grow and develop a fuller range of financial services.

A key limitation to the growth of a UK mortgage lender was the amount that they could lend out to households. If they depended only on their depositors, this placed a severe restriction on their lending. Deposits grew relatively slowly, whilst, of course, borrowers needed a large initial sum. One way around this was to tap into the wholesale money markets and borrow funds which they could then lend out. This involved short-term borrowing, perhaps for only a few weeks or months, but lending long-term, typically for 25 years. Clearly, this was a risky process, but the economic conditions in the late 1990s and early 2000s appeared sufficiently benign to allow for these tactics to work.

One of the most aggressive proponents of this tactic was the Newcastle-based former building society, Northern Rock (Brummer 2008; Turner 2008). It quite deliberately adopted a policy of rapid expansion based on wholesale funding. But also it was less discriminating in whom it would lend to, offering high loan-to-value mortgages, including what was known as the 'Together' loan which allowed young customers to borrow 125 per cent of the value of their property and at a multiple of six times their household income. This compared with the old industry standard of two-and-a-half times the household income and a loan limit of 75 per cent of the house value (Brummer 2008). As a result of these tactics Northern Rock expanded to the extent of providing 20 per cent of all UK mortgage lending in the first half of 2007 (Brummer 2008).

Whilst Northern Rock might have been exceptional in its aggressive lending, the whole UK financial system was going through a period of optimistic expansion. London was seen as the financial centre of the world, with its institutions at the forefront of innovation. As we have seen, this was something the Blair and Brown governments were more than willing to encourage. The new vibrant economy supposedly created by New Labour was to be based on services and new technologies rather than traditional industries. As a result the government adopted a position of light-touch regulation, particularly regarding large international financial institutions. New Labour took pride in creating a low-tax, low-regulation economy compared to other financial centres, and thus saw finance as an area of great success.

It was not, therefore, in a particularly strong position to warn against excessive risk. Indeed, the government was as keen to talk up the so-called 'new economic paradigm' as anyone else.

Northern Rock's business model depended on confidence, particularly on the part of the wholesale market. The problem by 2007, however, was that Northern Rock was rightly being seen as the closest thing in the UK to a sub-prime lender (Cable 2009). As confidence drained out of the US market, Northern Rock found that its funding was drying up and it became harder for it to service its debt on the wholesale market. In September 2007 the bank collapsed and called on government for support. This led to a run on the bank, the first in the UK for nearly 150 years, and the government was forced to underwrite all its deposits. Eventually the government was to lend up to £30 billion to Northern Rock and finally to nationalise it in early 2008. Northern Rock was followed later in 2008 by another demutualised building society, Bradford & Bingley, which was heavily committed to self-certified mortgages, whereby borrowers needed no proof of earnings, and the buy-to-let market.

Of course 2008 saw the globalisation of the debt crisis, going beyond the sub-prime mortgage markets in the US and UK. The US government was involved in several panic interventions to find buyers for financial institutions such as Bear Stearns (Cohan 2009) and Merrill Lynch. Perhaps most worryingly was the move of the Bush administration to effectively renationalise Fannie Mae and Freddie Mac and so potentially make the US taxpayer liable for $5.2 trillion of mortgage liabilities (Cable 2009).

In October 2008, the US government allowed one of the banks, Lehman Brothers, to collapse rather than bail it out. The result was a period of worldwide panic, in which several large international institutions seemed on the verge of collapse as trust and confidence drained from the system. What had seemed like a means of spreading risk across the global financial market now appeared like a net which was in danger of dragging down everyone. Risk appeared to have been magnified rather than dissipated across the system.

The UK and US governments responded to this crisis with a policy of seemingly limitless support, which in the cases of institutions like AIG, the largest insurance company in the world, and Halifax–Bank of Scotland (HBOS), the UK's largest mortgage lender, seemed to be urgently required. For a period in late 2008 the entire financial system seemed on the verge of collapse and at the time of writing (May–June 2009) it is by no means clear that the worst is over.

The outcome of this has been disastrous for housing markets in the UK and US. Scholtes (2009) shows that US house prices have fallen by more than 30 per cent from their 2005 peak. She shows that prices in California have fallen by 40 per cent and that 58 per cent of house sales in California in February 2009 involved foreclosures. In the UK, Goff (2009) reports that house prices in March 2009 had fallen by 17 per cent compared to the previous year.

While the decline in house prices might make houses more affordable – and interest rates are now at 0.5 per cent in the UK – many mortgage lenders have reversed their liberal lending policies and instead are now insisting on potential borrowers finding deposits of up to 30 per cent. This makes it particularly difficult for first-time buyers to gain access to the housing market. Birch (2009) shows how the UK market has changed since 2007. In September 2007 there were 2,583 mortgage products available to first-time buyers and 58 per cent of these products were available at 90–95 per cent of value. However, in March 2009 the number of available products had declined to 1,230, with only 5 per cent of these available at 90–95 per cent.

So the conditions in which households have to operate have changed markedly since 2006. Instead of a very liberal market in which access to finance was relatively easy, it is now much harder to gain access to housing. This is compounded by the reduction in new developments as housebuilders feel the effect of the recession on their sales and profitability (Pignal 2008).

## Conclusions

The situation in which individual households take their decisions about their housing has altered dramatically over the last few years. We have moved from a period of great optimism with regard to housing, during which individuals could justifiably feel more secure and affluent because of increasing house values, to one of extreme pessimism. We can see that much of the problem here is that what we take as personal and individual decisions are dependent on national and international factors, which occur regardless of our individual perspectives.

Individual households, who might now be faced with high levels of debt or negative equity or who cannot gain access to housing, are not stupid, nor have they been duped by some international conspiracy. Households have acted in what they perceived as their own best interests on the basis of the situation placed before them. Cheap finance was available for people who had a clear and important use for it. This appeared to be a profitable market and so it expanded as more players joined the market.

But we still must see the problem as in essence personal. We need to describe the problem in broad-brush terms, as I have done in this chapter, so that we can get something of a handle on the problem. But we should not forget the micro-level of a household aspiring to buy a property, of finding that the finance was made available and believing it was sensible and possible for them to purchase the house they wanted. They may have been wrong in their decision-making; they may not have had complete access to all the necessary information; they may not have known about the way in which mortgages were funded. This does not make them stupid. Rather it makes their situation tragic, because they are the ones who have suffered, who have lost everything. We can portray the sub-prime mortgage market as a scandal and point to the responsibility of agents, brokers and bankers, some of whom have since lost their jobs. They were well paid for their risk-taking and will recover. But not so those who lost their jobs, their houses and all that was in them.

The tendency to focus on the financial crisis as an aggregated entity – as one thing – is part of the very problem that led to the crisis. It is from this perspective that we see individual households as passive entities reacting to large impersonal forces. This also leads us to talk of 'the market' too as if it were itself one thing with a particular set of interests and incentives that can be predicted and modified. The key problem, I suggest, is that much of the problem has been the manner in which government, as a key player, has sought to understand and control markets. What we have seen, in the UK and the US, are governments which have sought to promote markets but have done so through a deliberately activist and interventionist approach. Government has clearly not understood markets but has rather allowed itself to be drawn into promoting particular interests as if they represented 'the market' as an entity. This is what I now turn to, not particularly to point the finger of blame so much as to help us understand just why things went so badly wrong.

# Chapter 4

# A political problem

## Introduction

Was the collapse of housing markets due to individual action? Of course no one is exactly forced to borrow money, even if it was cheap and offered to us on a plate, nor was it the borrowers who created the derivatives or securitised their loans and sold them on to others. It was not they who kept interest rates low and increased the supply of cheap credit. It was not individuals who argued it was easier to clear up a bubble after it had burst rather than deflate one.

But still, were individuals wrong to believe in the virtues of owner occupation as completely as they did? Was it not foolish – or worse – to assume that property was really that safe, and that we could use it as an investment, as well as a place to live? In response we might say that for any one household, there were, and still remain, clear benefits in owning their own dwelling: it made them feel more secure, they felt it was theirs, and so on. And of course each individual action, rational in its own terms, was of little consequence in itself. No one individual household or investor created the bubble or the consequent crash. Rather it was the combined actions of many in particular circumstances that created the problem.

A further difficulty is that no one acted in a manner that they thought would precipitate a collapse in housing markets and a worldwide recession. All households acted in a manner that they thought would be to their benefit. They might have been mistaken and might admit this in hindsight, but I would venture to suggest that many – perhaps the overwhelming majority – would not consider they had acted in error. Their actions in buying a house and spending the money they had earned and borrowed was sensible in its own terms and at the time it was done. None of these actions, taken on their own, was the cause of the recession.

Can we take the same view when it comes to the actions of governments and financial institutions? Are they more culpable? Many would say they are and point to overpaid – even greedy – bankers who took reckless risks, or to poor political and economic judgement on the part of politicians. But, again, can we claim that any institutions or government acted in a manner aimed at creating chaos? They acted in a manner that seemed best at the time.

Our task is made more complex still because there is a particular difficulty in trying to explain something whilst we are in the middle of it. We might think it would be better to wait until it was over, until housing markets have recovered and there is some stability again. But then one of the principal reasons for wanting to write in detail about a problem is to help solve it, and this means getting involved when it is actually happening. If we wish to provide credible remedies to housing boom and bust, we need to try to understand it whilst it is happening. This does, though, involve taking the risk that we may be missing something important, or even that the crisis develops in a particular manner that we cannot predict, and so we might find our musings irrelevant even before the ink is properly dry.

One way in which this has happened is the very manner in which the crisis is perceived. In 2006–7 it was seen primarily as a US problem based on the sub-prime housing market. This turned into a credit crunch as lending started to dry up, which in turn shifted the focus on to the solvency and liquidity of banks. We therefore, quite properly, saw this not as a housing problem, but as a financial one. However, in 2009, as the new Obama administration framed its first budget and the Brown government in the UK sought to explain how it planned to reduce the burgeoning budget deficit, the crisis began to be seen as being about debt, both private and public. The problem has therefore shifted from housing to banking to government and households. We might suggest that this is a question of changing emphasis as the crisis has developed, and it does not mean that the housing and financial aspects of the crisis have gone away, nor should we necessarily see these elements as being distinct. However, the emphasis that we place on the nature of the problem will obviously determine how we seek to deal with it.

Crises of the magnitude of those we have experienced since 2007 tend to have multiple causes. They occur as a result of many events, issues and circumstances coming together in a manner that could not be foreseen. It is seldom just one issue that remains dominant, even if we can point to something that set off the crisis, in this case the collapse of the sub-prime market in the US. Often the significance of each event is not clear at the time, but becomes evident only in hindsight. Sometimes we can see something as important almost immediately, as with the decision to let Lehman Brothers collapse in October 2008. But at other times it may be several years before we can properly assess the meaning of events. We must proceed cautiously and provisionally in seeking both explanations and remedies.

We should also beware of simplistic explanations that seek to provide a complete answer by recommending a thorough transformation of housing markets or even the entire international financial system. Some solutions can appear beguiling because they seem straightforward or are relatively easy to introduce. Other potential remedies may appeal because they suit particular ideological proclivities. Indeed there is a natural tendency to read the problem according to our own prejudices. For example, some see the crash as the fulfilment of their predictions of the end of capitalism, or at least the 'proof' that the Thatcher/Reagan era had failed. Accordingly, there has been something of a return to the pseudo-Keynesianism of the post-war era and even some suggesting stronger remedies. On the other hand, there are those worried that the proposed solution is more government when they see the problem as being caused in the first place by improper government action. Naturally, this is a somewhat harder argument to sustain, in that it appears to have been the bastions of free-market capitalism that failed. Also, with free-market views being seen to dominate over the last 30 years, it is hard to suggest that they might also be the remedy.

The argument that I pursue in this chapter is that we should see the problem not as one of failed capitalism, but of failing government. This is not because the model of capitalism that has dominated the global economy is perfect or without criticism. Rather, I argue that government has effectively operated according to a defective model of capitalism, whereby it has confused the interests of large corporate bodies with those of free markets. Governments in both the UK and US have operated a regulatory system that favours large financial institutions and has backed this up with activist government. In this way we have had the worst of both arguments discussed briefly above: we have had 'big' government operating a framework that favours corporatism rather than laissez-faire.

Any attempted explanation of the events of the last few years needs to take into account the various interests that were at play. Households, lenders and policy-makers have all had particular aims, which they must be considered to have held genuinely and sincerely, and which have helped to determine their actions. No events or outcomes were particularly inevitable or predetermined. Events might have gone differently and we should see the fact that the crisis was not predicted or pre-empted as evidence for this. Indeed, I suggest that much of the instability of housing markets has arisen because it was not in anyone's interest to point out the problems, let alone sort them out. Government has sought to promote and play on the popularity of owner occupation, and to benefit from a climate of cheap credit. It has needed private finance to fund public services and so relied upon effective and accessible credit markets. Households have benefited from cheap credit, low interest rates and appreciating asset values. There was a 'feel-good factor' which government sought to maintain by trying to manage housing markets. Lenders found the situation profitable, and the more they took risks the greater the profit that seemed to accrue. They sought to increase market share and found that the greater the risk, the higher the potential returns. None of these actions was particularly venal or aimed at creating instability; it was simply a matter of how interests which were devised separately came together.

This does not mean, however, that we cannot point to what went wrong and what should not have happened. What it does mean is that we cannot lay the blame at the door of one particular cause or suggest that changing one element – or even all elements – will have the desired effects.

In this chapter I seek to establish why things occurred as they did. I want to suggest that the cause was as much political as economic or financial. In the first part of the chapter I consider the role of government in promoting owner occupation, and try to assess what impact this has had. The second part then considers how far government can be seen as responsible for the crisis and whether other factors can mitigate any sense of blame. The final section introduces the concept of liberal corporatism as an explanation and links the politics of New Labour in the UK with the neo-conservatism of the Bush administration in the US.

## Owner occupation for all

Government intervention in housing is ubiquitous and influences actions and outcomes in very many ways. It can do this through the planning system, which can encourage or discourage supply and demand. This might involve the protection of certain places from being built on or through the use of planning gain. It might use subsidies which promote certain tenures or the interests of certain groups. These can take the form of capital subsidies to assist landlords in new development or housing allowances and tax exemptions for individuals. Government can regulate mortgage finance through the manipulation of interest rates or by insisting financial institutions maintain certain capital requirements. It might do this through the provision of mortgage insurance or by underwriting lending. Finally, it might also provide a statutory framework for the buying and selling of dwellings.

But this is by no means all that government can and does do. It might impose certain fitness standards in terms of what makes a dwelling uninhabitable or overcrowded. It might use rent regulation to alter the cost of housing for tenants, or it might impose a system of licensing for landlords to ensure standards. Governments are also not averse to using one tenure to support another, for example, in the case of the Right to Buy in the UK. These forms of intervention are interesting because they impose costs rather than benefits on particular players within the housing system.

This shows that housing markets do not lack government regulation and intervention and this has a number of purposes. It might seek to encourage certain tenures which are deemed to be popular or more socially beneficial. Intervention might be designed to make housing more affordable in general or for certain groups. Subsidies can have the effect of increasing supply and demand. But government might also wish to improve public health and make housing safer for residents by the imposition of certain standards. Government might also wish to increase economic activity by promoting construction and therefore employment.

Governments act because they wish to create change, and we must assume, in democratic, open societies at least, that they act for the best of motives. Governments are accountable to their electorates and to public opinion more generally. Housing policy is not, generally speaking, conducted in secret, but is a public process in which each step tends to be announced in advance and so is open to comment and conjecture. But still some forms of government intervention can have perverse consequences: for example, rent regulation, which reduced the supply of good-quality dwellings, and planning controls, which can create scarcity and higher prices (King 2009). It might be that some of these costs are deemed to be a reasonable trade-off, in that higher standards are beneficial, even if the cost is higher and supply is reduced somewhat. But there are other occasions when the consequences would neither be expected nor particularly desired.

As we have seen in the discussion on boom and bust in Chapter 3, government action can clearly be implicated in the collapse of housing markets. Governments have sought to promote owner occupation over a considerable period in the UK and US. This has undoubtedly been a popular policy and one which large sections of the respective electorates have been comfortable with. But, in the light of the collapse of housing markets, is government intervention, particularly its support of owner occupation, correct and justified?

At the time of writing (May–June 2009) there is a scandal in the UK over the manner in which members of Parliament have been claiming expenses, particularly those related to their housing costs. Several MPs, including some very senior ministers, appear to have been using taxpayers' money to improve a dwelling and then selling this dwelling at a considerable profit free from tax. Whilst this was within the rules which MPs themselves approved, it is increasingly seen as illegitimate. But, might we not see this tactic, whereby public money is used to subsidise an appreciating asset that the owner may then profit from, as rather more common? All those who have used the Right to Buy have a potential capital gain at the state's expense, as do those who have claimed tax relief on their mortgage interest.

Whatever the view that the British public has towards its MPs, there has been no attempt to connect the specific issue of parliamentarians making a profit with the more general situation of gaining from a public subsidy of their housing. This being so, on what grounds can subsidising owner occupation ever be justified? Why is it not a clear principle that we should not subsidise owner occupation on the grounds that the recipients will then have an asset of increasing value, which they can then benefit from?

On one level we might see this situation in pragmatic terms. It is something that we are used to. UK households do not pay tax on the sale of their residence because it is simply not the thing we do. Likewise, US households get tax relief on interest payments because that is just how the world is. Owner occupation in both countries is now so dominant that any challenge to this is very difficult. It is true that tax relief on mortgage interest (MITR) was abolished in the UK in 2000, but this was after the subsidy had been allowed to atrophy, not having been increased since 1983 (King 2001). Even so, the relief was phased out over five years, with no changes in 1997 because of the general election due that year.

We might suggest that the support for owner occupation is rooted in political opportunism, but this opportunism can quickly become political necessity, especially when a government or representatives are facing re-election. The problem is that when owner occupation has become as large as it has in the UK and the US, with over two-thirds of households enjoying the tenure, it becomes politically difficult if not impossible to oppose it. When we are in a situation in which the majority expect to remain or become owner occupiers, and who see no viable alternative, it takes a strong government not to be swayed. It becomes difficult, if not impossible, for government to withhold support for the tenure or to suggest that it has any natural limits. Governments in the UK have consistently argued that owner occupation can and should be expanded (DOE 1995; DETR 2000; CLG 2007). For a government to say that owner occupation is at saturation point is to suggest that those not currently in owner occupation ought not to become owners. It would be to say that owner occupation is only for certain types and that the opportunity can be denied to others.

So the issue is not just that governments have consistently supported owner occupation, but also the manner in which these supports have developed and whom they have been increasingly targeted at. In both the UK and US there have been concerted attempts over the last two decades to promote owner occupation, not just to the affluent middle classes, but to all households. US lenders have faced increasing pressure to provide funding to low-income households, often on the quite understandable grounds of dealing with discrimination against racial minorities. In the UK the support for owner occupation has taken on a social justice rhetoric (King 2006) with the initiative Homes for All (ODPM, 2005) and the development of low-cost home ownership (LCHO), key-worker housing, HomeBuy, and so on. The 2007 green paper (CLG, 2007) spoke of using social housing as a ladder into owner occupation, and of pathways to home ownership. The idea seemed to be to spread owner occupation as widely as possible. The middle classes enjoy it so why should the working classes and low-income households be left out?

Such a policy is undoubtedly popular and so support for owner occupation becomes a political and electoral necessity. But is it sensible? For example, does it make sense for successive US governments to insist that mortgages be offered equally to all parts of the community? We might wish to see that all households have access to financial services so that they are able to play a full part in society and the economy. But actually legislating for equal access assumes that the risks of lending to all parts of the community are equal, when in fact certain households are inherently less suitable. This is not because they are morally deficient, nor is it due to any discrimination. Rather it is because households that live in areas with higher levels of crime, who have lower incomes or insecure employment, are less reliable as borrowers. Legislation to ensure financial inclusion alters the risk structures and incentives of financial institutions. By forcing them to lend, financial institutions have either to charge more for these high-risk groups, as was the case with sub-prime mortgages, or seek to spread the cost across all their borrowers and thereby subsidise the poor risks.

We can suggest that one of the outcomes of this attempt at financial inclusion has been the creative engineering of financial products, such as sub-prime mortgages and their derivatives. Lenders had an increased incentive to pass on risk to other financial institutions who sought to benefit from the risk premium charged to sub-prime borrowers. But the effect of this was to create a market that depended on lending to high-risk households and being able to pass on that risk and continue to move it. The attempt to help low-income households into owner occupation created a market for risk which quickly enmeshed the world's financial markets. The result, when these loans started to go bad, was a chain reaction that left many millions of households considerably worse off, with governments having to support the entire financial system for fear of a catastrophic meltdown.

We can question here whether the problem was actually one of extending owner occupation, or whether it was rather due to the financial engineering that led to sub-prime mortgages being sliced and diced and then traded around the world. Was it a matter of system design rather than anything intrinsic to the product? We might argue that sub-prime mortgages were always likely to be problematic because of the need for low interest rates and continued house price inflation. Lending money to people with limited resources is inherently more risky. However, certain policies have worked well in assisting large numbers of low-income households into owner occupation, particularly the Right to Buy in the UK (King 2010). But we need to be aware that this policy has worked so successfully only because of the special circumstances that underpinned the policy: there was an existing stock of dwellings, in the form of council housing; it was possible to use the free equity in the dwellings to provide substantial discounts at nil cost to central government; there was a sufficient number of capable households (and indeed the scheme was never for the very poorest); and it was a scheme that was simple to understand and to sell. These circumstances cannot be easily replicated, as has become apparent with other schemes, such as HomeBuy, which are complex, less advantageous to potential households and on a much smaller scale because of the expense involved (King 2009, 2010). What we might conclude, therefore, is that unless government has a particular set of advantageous circumstances, as was the case with the Right to Buy, it is difficult to envisage a means of assisting low-income households into owner occupation without a high level of risk. And in a situation like that of the US, in which risk was being borne to some extent by lenders, it is not surprising that means were sought to transfer that risk.

The situation is compounded because there are now so few alternatives to owner occupation. Indeed, in the UK this can be seen as the first housing recession of the age of mass owner occupation. The possible alternatives, be it private renting or social housing, are now so marginalised, and owner occupation so dominant, that the only answer to housing markets that do not work are housing markets that do. The issue, quite simply, is that most households have nowhere else to go but owner occupation. Social housing, which makes up 18 per cent of dwellings, is allocated according to priority need and, needless to say, is already fully occupied. Social housing could only become an alternative were there to be a massive house-building programme by government. Yet there seems to be little prospect of a more balanced pattern of tenure as exists in Germany and the Netherlands. Some may regret this, but there is simply no possibility of government funding a building programme necessary to dramatically alter the position.

We can demonstrate this quite quickly by looking at some figures. If we take the rather conservative assumption that a new dwelling in the social housing sector costs £100,000 to build, and if government sought to assist all those currently on social landlords' housing lists, which is reported to be 2.5 million households, the cost would be £250 billion. This is an absurd figure in terms of what government has been spending on housing over the last decade (between £5 billion and £7 billion per annum) and would remain so even if half the cost were to be raised from private finance (which of course might prove difficult in the current financial climate). The Brown government has responded to the collapse in housing markets by increasing spending on social housing in 2009 by £1 billion, but has been able to do so only by bringing forward money allocated for 2010–12. At the current rate of spending, we are therefore talking in terms of several generations to fund building on the scale required to meet current unmet needs, even if government were to redirect all its housing expenditure to new building. Any major change in tenure patterns would be the work of generations, and so would be irrelevant as a response to a recession. Indeed the decline of social renting has taken place over a 30-year period and any return to a large council housing sector would be likely to take just as long. The only alternative to this would involve the mass confiscation of private property by national or local government. But this would not increase the total size of the housing stock, even if we could take such an event as politically tenable (but then the idea that the US government would nationalise banks and insurance companies would have seemed absurd in 2007).

The point of this discussion is not to suggest a viable programme – of course government is not going to build millions of new dwellings in the social housing sector – but rather to show the particular situation that a country like the UK (and the US) is in. Any practical alternative to the dominance of owner occupation is not tenable in anything but the very long term.

Even if it could be afforded, it seems unlikely to be supported politically. We could question if many would actually accept a return to renting. Owner occupation is now something we see as natural. We expect to own our housing, so we can use it how we like, move when we want, and so on. This being so, why would we accept going back to renting? Social housing has what we might term an image problem. It is something that households use when they fall on hard times and really have no other alternative; it is for 'other people', for people 'not like us'. This attitude might be considered unfortunate, reprehensible even, but it exists and it is something that politicians are acutely aware of. The mentality towards renting in the UK has changed so fundamentally since the 1970s that it is hard to contemplate any alternative. Of course such a transformation is possible: change occurs and the unforeseen happens. But, as we have seen, in tenure terms things can change only very slowly, and this applies as much to the perception of social housing as to its size.

This leads us back to the question of whether politicians were wrong to support owner occupation. The policies pursued by them have helped to cause a housing boom followed by a bust, and so in that sense we can argue that they might have been wrong. But in mitigation, these policies were clearly what many people wanted. Politicians could legitimately argue they had a mandate to promote owner occupation, as well as a long history of support to emulate. It fitted clear cultural expectations towards greater property ownership. Of course we might argue that politicians are there to do what is right and not merely what is popular. The problem, however, is that the 'rightness' of a particular course of action can be known only in the future, whilst popularity exists in the present. In any case, asking what is right is not exactly an objective question, but is rather dependent on what one sees as the proper role of government and political action. A libertarian's conception of what is right would not concur with that of a Marxist, and neither would necessarily accept that the issue could be determined solely by empirical criteria.

In as much as we might argue that no one would wish there to be a recession, we might argue that no one would 'invent' the housing systems that existed in the UK and US in 2007. However, we are not capable of starting from anywhere else but where we currently find ourselves, and the cultural and political conditions that now pertain cannot be wished away. This does not necessarily exonerate anyone, but it does temper the way in which we view those who might be responsible, and it is this issue of responsibility that I tackle next.

## So is government to blame?

In the aftermath of the banking crisis in October 2008 politicians, the press and the general public sought people to blame, and much of the responsibility fell on the bankers themselves. Stories of apparent greed and venality filled the newspapers and the airwaves as the actions of bankers – and their salaries and bonuses – were subjected to close and hostile scrutiny. Without wishing to exonerate anyone – I too would appreciate a gold-plated pension fund for my proven incompetence – the bankers were a very easy target. They were the public face of the crisis, since they were the ones who had taken the last set of decisions that led to it.

Yet the problem, as I have suggested in Chapter 3, is rather more deep-seated than that. In particular, this has been by no means the only example of housing boom and bust in recent history. In the UK, we can point to similar examples in the early 1970s and the late 1980s/early 1990s as just the most recent examples. But if we know that booms and busts have happened before, why could we not foresee this one and prevent it? The easy answer to this is greed and/or stupidity, but this would imply that these vices were extremely widespread and that all the clever people running banks and governments were either deluded or liars.

In general terms, we can point to a number of reasons for the failure to prevent the boom and bust from happening despite the existence of many previous examples to learn from. First, we might argue that the post-2006 crisis was different from those that preceded it and so it could not be predicted. But whilst there are no exact parallels with past events, we can say that there were sufficient similarities – rapid house price inflation, supply shortages, cheap finance – to suggest that things were not as benign as many were arguing.

Second, and more plausibly, whilst such events have happened in the past, they tend to occur sufficiently infrequently to ensure that there are different people in charge of companies and the country when the next one happens. Indeed, as we saw in 2008, the first casualties of the bust were the senior executives of financial institutions, who were the very ones with the most experience. This means that the next cycle starts with new people at the helm and the most experienced players discredited.

Third, we can argue that it was in no one's particular interest to change what was happening. The direction of travel appeared to be in the short- to medium-term interests of politicians, bankers and households. Politicians argued that the boom was a permanent change in economic reality; the banks were profiting handsomely from their invention; and households were making significant paper gains from increasing house values. Whilst there were some politicians and commentators who were worried about the situation and tried to call attention to the problems of increasing indebtedness and government spending, they were very much in the minority and lacked a sufficient constituency to be listened to.

Fourth, we can argue that no one, be they optimist or pessimist, had the complete picture. Households and politicians were not aware of what the bankers were up to with their creation of new and complex financial products, and nor were governments always open about their finances, just as many households were not always open about theirs. Finally, there is the problem of following the herd. If everyone was playing this particular game, what alternatives were there? Financial institutions felt the need to compete with other institutions in order not to be left behind in terms of profits and market share; politicians saw a ready link between economic growth and political popularity; and households saw what could be made from property or felt the need to buy whilst they could afford to.

All these factors point to a situation of drifting into a crisis with no incentive to change. But does that mean that no one was to blame? In particular, can we point to actions by governments that were, albeit in hindsight, wrong or misguided? The role of government is important because only it can change laws, raise and lower taxes, and control the levers of monetary and fiscal policy. Government therefore provides the context in which households and financial institutions operate. So it is reasonable to look at the actions of government to see if it helped to precipitate the crisis.

The first and most obvious factor was that governments in both the UK and US ensured that credit was cheap and readily accessible with interest rates set at historically low levels. Indeed, unlike previous recessions, this one was not the result of inflation and the need to tighten monetary policy. Rather it was the case of monetary policy being kept loose as a deliberate tactic to maintain levels of credit (Booth 2009). This leads on to the second factor: governments and central bankers had the apparently sincere belief that a bubble could be controlled, and that it was more effective to clear up the fallout of what was thought to be a controlled boom than try to stop it whilst still in progress. This was certainly the view of Alan Greenspan, the chairman of the US Federal Reserve. The result was that the boom was funded not by domestic saving, but by borrowing. But as the regulators argued they could control the economy, this was not seen as problematic and the trend towards the use of credit was further encouraged. Linked to this policy was the belief, again argued by Greenspan (2007), that markets were self-stabilising and so changes in the economy could be compensated for. This meant that there was no need for government to intervene.

As we saw in Chapter 3, governments over many years have offered practical and rhetorical support for owner occupation, which both built on the desire people had to own and helped to maintain it. The actions of government, particularly when it came to encouraging low-income households into owner occupation, gave the impression that the tenure was for everyone and that no one should be excluded. In this sense the rhetoric matched the policy of loose monetary policy.

But there was a further issue that is important in explaining the role of government in boom and bust. Governments in the UK and US wanted loose monetary policy not merely to encourage households to borrow, but also because they had themselves become dependent on borrowing to fund their expenditure. The Bush administration borrowed to fund its wars and tax cuts, whilst the Blair/Brown governments used borrowing to fund their massive increase in spending on the public services. So government was not in a position to lecture others on the dangers of over-borrowing, even if it had been prepared to acknowledge the dangers.

The final point, which we shall discuss more fully in the next section, is that both governments in both the UK and US, despite their rhetoric in support of markets and enterprise, were very activist. Indeed, in the UK at least, there was a rather hubristic attitude shown by senior members of the government. Gordon Brown, in particular, appeared to consider himself uniquely competent to control the UK economy. The result of this was a lack of corporate decision-making and accountability. It may be coincidence, but both the governments in the UK and US had been in power for a considerable period (Bush for seven years; Blair/Brown for 10) and so there may have been a degree of complacency or even tiredness about them.

For all this apparent culpability these were elected governments doing, broadly speaking, what they were elected to do. Indeed, whilst both governments suffered periods of unpopularity due to wars going wrong and to particular scandals, their policies towards owner occupation were by no means unsupported. Both governments were going with the grain of public opinion by trying to make owner occupation more affordable and opening up the tenure to all.

So what we might argue is that government created a series of conditions which made a boom and bust more likely. It did not control the action of either households or banks, but it did create conditions in which excessive risks could be taken in the apparent belief that they were reasonable. Perhaps what we could say is that the fault on the part of government was in not maintaining the necessary safety margin, but instead encouraging a climate of speculation and risk-taking on the part of households and financial institutions.

The issue of responsibility and blame does not just relate to causes, but also consequences and, in particular, how government seeks to deal with the aftermath of boom and bust. It appears that a crisis created, at least partially, by government action can be dealt with only by more government action. This, as we shall see in the next section, is a particular quality shared by both the Bush and Blair/Brown governments. They both believe in active interventionism, and the events of 2008 and after have not shaken that belief.

We can see this as being at least partly political, in that governments are seeking to maintain their positions, particularly in the UK where the serving Prime Minister, Gordon Brown, was the principal architect of light regulation and is seeking to reinvent himself as the creator of a new global financial architecture. Of paramount importance to the Brown government is to shift the responsibility – more specifically, any sense of blame – onto anything or anyone but him. Brown is at a considerable disadvantage in this compared to the Obama administration in the US, which took office in January 2009 and cannot be held to account for what happened before then. Brown, however, has been the dominant figure in UK economic and domestic policy since 1997 and so any problems are harder to displace.

The problem in the UK is that it is difficult to undertake a drastic change in policy without the implication of admitting to serious errors made in the past. Obama can change policies on the basis of his new mandate and blame his predecessor in the process. In the UK, any means to deal with the financial crisis have to be undertaken without the suggestion that serious policy errors might have been made between 1997 and 2007. This has meant that the UK government has had to invest heavily in the notion that the crisis is global in nature and that its provenance is external to Britain. Britain, as it were, has been caught off guard by events not of its own making. Therefore, the role that the Brown administration has tried to construct for itself is of a resolute government taking the necessary tough decisions to defend the British economy in the face of the unforeseen.

There is an assumption that one of the roles of government is to smooth out unintended consequences. Ideally it should prevent them but, if not, then deal with their effects (Williams 1997). However, we need to remember that government is not a neutral actor: it too has interests, both as a whole and within the different parts of government, and it takes decisions accordingly. Government acts in a short-term and parochial fashion like any individual or firm, and this tends to happen all the more as an election approaches. What makes this dangerous is that government can make laws and raise taxes and, in the UK, has the ability to determine the date of an election. But, despite these powers, government has proven to be no more prescient than any other player and is as equally bound by self-interest and parochial concerns. Governments across the world could not prevent the credit crunch in 2007, and in the UK the Brown government went to particular lengths to deny the possibility of a recession until it became inevitable in late 2008. Indeed the response of the Brown government to the developing crisis has been particularly enlightening. First, Brown stated consistently that there would be no return to boom and bust, even going so far as to guarantee the fact. When the downturn started, we were told there would be no recession. This changed into a story that the recession would not be severe and that Britain was particularly well placed to ride out the economic problems as a result of its low levels of debt. However, a fiscal stimulus was then necessary in November 2008 to 'save' the banking system and there was further talk of another stimulus in the April 2009 Budget. By early 2009 it had become clear that another stimulus was unaffordable because of the state of the public finances, so the government claimed it had already done enough stimulating and the emphasis began to shift to how it could maintain essential public services and plan for a reduction in debt. The only consistent element of this changing narrative was that nothing that had happened could have been foreseen by government and so it could not be held responsible for it. At each stage the government tried to provide a consistent narrative of active government, of government being the only agent capable of leading the country out of recession. Yet the reality was of a government capable only of reacting to and chasing rather than controlling the agenda.

So we can suggest that many of the Brown government's actions since 2007 have been about blame displacement and showing Brown himself in a favourable light: one in which he can be seen to be saving the situation, but not to have caused it, even though he had been in charge of economic policy since 1997. The pursuit of the government's interests, parochial as they are, has dominated the response to the crisis. For example, borrowing for recurrent spending on public services and increased expenditure on welfare benefits due to increasing unemployment has been recast as an economic stimulus, even though a considerable part of this spending was planned. Public spending, at the levels planned during the boom, appears to be sacrosanct, with the only change being in how they are justified. Likewise, institutions created by Brown, particularly the Financial Services Authority, which proved ineffective in regulating banks, cannot be reformed or abolished as this would reflect back on Brown's judgement.

A further attempt at blame displacement was the manner in which the UK government sought to portray government debt. It portrayed Britain as being in a more favourable position compared to countries like Japan and Italy, which have a national debt well in excess of 100 per cent of GDP: the practice under Brown had been to maintain debt at below 40 per cent. However, this favourable position could be maintained only by describing government debt in a particular manner. The Brown government tended to describe government debt as a stock, and so referred only to the accumulated national debt, which, as we have seen, was relatively low compared to other states. However, where we describe debt as a flow, which would relate to the government's current income and expenditure, we would see that this had been consistently in deficit for most of the period since 2000. Referring to debt as a stock put the government's position in a good light and allowed Brown to argue that debt was low and therefore the government had considerable leeway in its actions compared to the governments of other countries. But to focus on the flow of debt would have made it clear that the UK had a structural budget deficit not caused by the recession, but due to imprudent government spending on the public sector since 2000. This means that government public spending had been excessive relative to income for a number of years and could be maintained only by borrowing. In effect, the government had been borrowing in a boom rather than creating surpluses to deal with a downturn in the economic cycle. The result is that were the recession to end immediately, the public debts would still be considerable. The recession, and the need to stimulate the economy, is therefore being used as a means to maintain existing levels of expenditure, even though it is technically unaffordable. The result is a burgeoning public debt with borrowing accounting for about £1 in every £5 spent by government.

The Obama administration is not blamed for the recession but it still has to deal with the consequences of its predecessor, and this involves dealing with government debt whilst trying to stimulate the economy out of recession. Even here we can see a more covert agenda, with parts of the Obama stimulus package relating to what may well turn out to be permanent spending, such as on health care and employment initiatives. This spending is actually part of the Democrats' long-term policy agenda and is not specifically related to dealing with a housing or a financial crisis.

In one sense, we might accept that government did not cause the crisis. If it is ineffectual in pre-empting it or clearing it up, why should we assume it could cause it? Is it not inconsistent to argue that government is powerful enough to mess things up, but not to clear up the mess? Are we being unfair on government by effectively taking the opposite of Brown's view? Instead of government being innocent of blame, yet uniquely competent to sort it out, is there not a danger of assuming that government is solely to blame, yet cannot sort it out? But the issue is not really about power: government has certainly accreted to itself the ability to control much of the economy and it certainly has the tools at its disposal (Jenkins 1995; King 2006). What is rather at issue is whether government can understand what is happening and therefore what impact its actions actually have. Government has powers over taxation and spending – over £600 billion in 2009/10 in the UK; it can change laws and constitutions; it can create and abolish agencies and institutions; and it can confiscate property as well as sell off its own assets. But this does not mean that any government fully understands what it is doing.

This suggests that it is easier for government to do harm than good. It is easy for government to change something, but this does not mean that it can predict what will happen as a result. Accordingly, we might argue that government should seek to limit its actions so that, first and foremost, it makes sure that it does no harm. The powers that government has – to tax and spend, create and abolish, confiscate and give away – should mean that it acts with extreme caution and only if it is fully aware of the effects of its actions. A particular example of this form of action was the Brown government's attempt in late 2008 to encourage lenders to borrow again at 2007 levels, that is to say, before the credit crunch and collapse in UK housing markets. This would suggest that housing markets could be restored to their former level, and the government could then say that the problem was solved, well in time for re-election at that. However, within six months this argument was forgotten because it had become all too clear from the level of personal, corporate and government debt that the damage could not be so easily undone. Only then did government start to come to terms with the significance of indebtedness. Still the attitude of the Brown government, to misquote St Augustine, appeared to be 'Make me thrifty, Lord, but not yet.'

The issue here was that the government was seeking a short-term political means to deal with the crisis. But, in doing so, it showed that it was still wedded to the notion of supporting the expansion of owner occupation and restoring housing markets. It could not break from the mentality that the proper role of government was to protect and support the popular tenure, even if this meant ignoring the underlying issues of public and private debt. The attitude of government was that the way to deal with the problem was merely to do more of the same.

A similar argument is presented by governments with regard to public spending. As we have seen, both the UK and US governments are averse to reducing public spending. Indeed they have argued that the way to deal with a financial crisis caused in part by indebtedness and over-consumption is for government to increase the level of spending, so that the public compensates for the private. But why should we assume that the cause of the problem will also cure it?

In any case, is the distinction between public and private debt a particularly valid one? Private debt is a personal responsibility, in that we have to use our own income to clear the debt or we have to take the consequences. The responsibility is ours; we have voluntarily taken on a particular commitment, such as borrowing to buy a house. If we are unable to meet these commitments, then the consequences to us are clear and known. We can suggest that actions taken against us are reasonable, even if they are deeply distressing and even traumatic.

But public debt operates differently. We may portray it as government debt, as that which is owed by government. But this is not really the case, as the government can only gain access to any money through the taxation of private income. If the government needs to increase its income to fund its debts, then it must increase taxation from its citizens. Therefore public debt affects the general public. But, except in the indirect sense of taking part in elections, the public has not been party to the decision to borrow. The governments of the UK and US did not ask permission from its citizens to borrow. It might have had support for its wars (initially, at least), or claim a mandate for tax cuts and increased expenditure on health care, but it did not say that this spending would be unfunded. The result of government debt is that every taxpayer becomes responsible. The liability falls on the taxpayer, not the particular agency itself.

Likewise, the manner in which government might seek to deal with its debts, through inflation or printing money, are avenues not open to private individuals, but which impact directly on all citizens, regardless of their support for any government. The debts of government become ours and so we can say that the effects of public debt go much wider than private debt, falling on all members of society, as do any attempts to remedy the situation. Therefore we can point to clear differences in responsibility and accountability between public and private debt. Or rather that the same agents – private individuals – become responsible for both public and private debt.

The role of government, therefore, is crucial in understanding the most recent housing boom and bust. Its actions are particularly consequential, and so there is some clear need for us to be aware of what impact government can have, both in terms of causing a crisis, and also, as we shall discuss more fully in Chapter 5, in helping to sort it out. But before moving on to look at remedies, there is still one important issue left unresolved. We have considered what government did and have sought some political explanations for it. However, we must investigate the particular nature of those governments in the US and UK to explain the apparent paradox of an active government seeking to promote private interests and enterprise. In other words, if both the UK and US governments were so market friendly, how did they create such a mess?

## Liberal corporatism

When New Labour was elected in 1997, it brought with it a new rhetoric for government, what it termed a 'third way' (Blair 1998) between old-fashioned socialism and traditional conservatism. New Labour sought to meld together social justice with entrepreneurialism to create a new style of politics and economics. It was very much in favour of new paradigms and a jargon of transformation based on the adoption of elements from Left and Right. We might characterise its position as 'purposive perversity', whereby it sought to achieve its political aims through the partial adoption of the approach of its opponents. It disavowed the Labour Party's traditional beliefs and deliberately alienated some of the Party's more vociferous traditional supporters. The aim was to prove that the Party had changed fundamentally from how it was previously perceived, and so could be trusted with government. But this also served to disarm political opponents who found that their best lines had been stolen. Accordingly, New Labour adopted a pro-market approach, using the rhetoric of laissez-faire as a means of separating itself from the failures of Old Labour.

The problem, however, was that New Labour did not necessarily understand markets and capitalism any better merely
because of the rhetoric it adopted and the new friends it made.
Indeed, instead of understanding markets and how they operate,
New Labour seemed to assume that siding with the interests of
big business and personal wealth was the same as being
supportive of free markets. It seemed to assume that corporate
interests were the same as those of a free economy. Accordingly,
the government adopted a light-touch regulatory framework by
establishing the Financial Services Authority, chose to ignore tax
loopholes that favoured the interests of international business and
finance, and so made the City of London a centre for speculative
finance. New Labour, keen to free itself from dependency on
union funding, had become comfortable with wealth creation.

This did not mean that markets were working any better, or
that Blair and Brown had a sophisticated understanding of
capitalism. The structures they developed might not be seen as
capitalistic so much as 'socialism for big business', whereby large
corporations were supported by government and given a
relatively free hand, even as other sectors of the economy were
being regulated and controlled using minimum wage legislation
and the Human Rights Act, and by rigorously applying EU regulations. Large companies could deal with this form of regulation
more readily because of their global span. They could bear the
additional costs through diversification across jurisdictions and
by moving activities offshore. Smaller firms, based in specific
communities, were not so advantaged, but found themselves
increasingly incapable of competing with international players.

Throughout their period in office New Labour persisted with
what might be called a 'public sector mentality', even as it
supported the private sector and markets. It still had the benign
acceptance of the role of government as competent and the
proper agency to deal with most of society's problems. New
Labour may have had a desire to free itself from the unions
and find alternative sources of funding; it may have seen socialism
as old fashioned and stopped referring to itself as socialist; it
may have adopted a new vocabulary for politics, a new discourse
which was able to connect the Party with the changed

environment in which it found itself. However, this did not mean a fundamental change in mentality. New Labour still sought to manage the economy from the centre. With the possible exception of Prime Minister Blair, the background of New Labour politicians was fairly typical in that they were rooted in socialist ideas and history. Some senior cabinet ministers had indeed been on the extreme Left in their younger days. What had altered was a need to reconnect with the mainstream after the transformation engineered by Mrs Thatcher and the Conservatives in the 1980s and 1990s. The result was a denial of socialist rhetoric, but this did not manifest itself in any change of attitude towards government. New Labour certainly did not act in a socialist way but it retained a socialist mentality of active and interventionist government.

We might see that much of the New Labour period of government was based on something of an illusion: the pro-market rhetoric favoured big business but hid an active programme of government intervention. This, however, proved to be deeply problematic, in that government was in a situation of seeking to promote the public sector and certain private interests at the same time, and to convince the electorate that there was no contradiction here. Accordingly, the government increasingly chose to fund public-sector projects, such as building schools and hospitals, not out of general taxation, but by using private finance and by developing off-balance sheet techniques, such as the Private Finance Initiative, which hid the true cost of the government's commitments. In addition, as we have seen, it turned to borrowing to maintain its expenditure and keep taxes at historically low levels. But, despite the use of these techniques and continual talk of reform and efficiency, there was no real deregulation of the public sector or opening it up to competition. Instead, spending increased. Deregulation occurred only in the financial sector to the benefit of large corporations, who were averse, in any case, to competition.

New Labour was not prepared to present the public with the true costs of its actions, whilst continuing to proclaim the possibility of heightened choice and the benefits of competition. The position was sustainable only so long as economic growth was maintained, house prices continued to rise and households felt more affluent. Once that situation altered with the recession after 2007, the government found itself severely limited. As a result of the rhetoric of New Labour, Prime Minister Brown was forced into a position such that it was impossible to make large cuts in public expenditure, but had no revenue stream to fund it. The government found it impossible to suggest that continued public spending was now a social evil, just as it could not suggest that its management of the financial sector was in any way deficient. The rhetoric and policies of New Labour were based entirely on a growing economy that allowed for the expansion of credit and thus the continuation of public and private expenditure at ever higher levels. This was the only means of keeping the two sides of the New Labour coalition – corporate finance and the public sector – together. Once economic growth stopped and the country entered recession, the contradictions at the heart of New Labour's tactics became all too apparent. However, no alternative means of progressing could be countenanced precisely because this would show the intellectual paucity at the heart of the New Labour project.

The illusion perpetrated by New Labour was successful, but ultimately problematic, because of how it seemed to fit with a range of interests. The government was able to develop the illusion of prudence and competence because its policies seemed to work to everyone's advantage. Private households were able to accumulate at least paper wealth on the back of cheap housing finance. The public sector saw expanded budgets and greater influence, with a considerable increase in the public payroll. Finally, the financial sector was buoyed by the housing market and encouraged to take risks and increase short-term profitability. All of this seemed to benefit the government politically and electorally, enabling New Labour to maintain a considerable constituency in terms of votes, funding and political support.

This constituency consisted of a mix of personal choice and aspiration with an enlarged public sector funded both by direct government expenditure and by private finance. However, the problem with this mix of the public and private was that there was no internal means of constraint. Indeed each element seemed to feed on the other to create a rather toxic cocktail once the economic prospects changed. New Labour created a coalition of public and private irresponsibility that worked, in the short term at least, for the mutual benefit of politicians, bankers and households, but which in time created the conditions for a massive collapse in housing markets and a recession in the wider economy. Financial institutions were encouraged into ever greater corporate risk-taking, particularly their use of the wholesale debt market. We saw the consequences of this when we discussed Northern Rock in Chapter 3. But, in addition, there was an increase in domestic borrowing to fund higher housing and private expenditure, and this was matched by government over-spending and hubris based on short-term political ends.

So far we have concentrated on the UK, but there are a number of similarities with the situation that pertained in the US. New Labour was initially close to the Clinton administration, which seemed to share much of the 'third way' rhetoric and the need for a new settlement that saw the centre-left acceptance of markets. What was interesting, however, was the manner in which New Labour retained close links with the Bush administration, which came to office in 2001. Bush, despite his conservative image, was similar in mentality to Blair and Brown in the UK. As Gershon (2007) points out, Bush was not libertarian in his outlook, but rather believed in strong government action to achieve certain aims. There was indeed some disjuncture between the apparent cosmopolitan sophistication of New Labour and the homespun Texan common sense of Bush, yet there were ready similarities in their approach to government. Indeed we have already pointed to some of these, particularly the light-touch regulation of business and finance, and the encouragement of owner occupation, particularly extending to low-income groups. Both governments were also committed to huge increases in public expenditure and consequent increase in public debt. And they both used a rhetoric of support for free markets and personal choice.

Of course Bush can be seen as neo-conservative in outlook, whilst New Labour was ostensibly left of centre. However, even a cursory look at the history of neo-conservatism shows some similarities with New Labour. The early neo-conservatives, such as Irving Kristol and Gertrude Himmelfarb, were Trotskyites in the 1930s, who slowly drifted from the extreme left through the Democratic Party to become Republican supporters of Reagan and the second Bush (Heilbrunn 2008; Kristol 1995). Heilbrunn (2008) argues that even though the neo-conservatives moved dramatically away from their leftist roots, they did not change their basic attitude towards politics, which was based on direct action and principle over pragmatism.

Whilst neo-conservatism was never imported with any great success into the UK, it is interesting that an important collection of neo-conservative writings prepared at the height of the movement's influence in 2004 (Stelzer 2004) includes a speech on liberal interventionism by Tony Blair. This might suggest that the links between Bush and New Labour were based mainly on foreign policy and the war on terror, but I believe that the roots go rather deeper and relate to a shared disposition that government action can have positive results and is to be preferred to the private actions of individuals. It is easy to create a connection between neo-conservatism and New Labour through the war in Iraq and the shared values of liberal interventionism, but rather what is in play here is a shared model of political economy. Europeans describe this as Anglo-Saxon, which may be accurate but is not terribly descriptive; perhaps better would be liberal corporatism. Government seeks to use the levers at its command to achieve ends compatible with markets, but in doing so seeks to maintain a high degree of control. This is essentially leftist in its ambitions for government, but in neither the UK nor the US did it meet particularly leftist aims. Here we have a linkage based not so much on overt ideology as the processes of political action and the means of achieving political change. What was in common was an approach to government action and how personal choice and aspiration could be linked to a programme of political action. There was a shared ideal that individuals could be helped to achieve their aspirations by a benign government. The result can be seen as a form of safety net, or an underwriting of private actions.

The connection between New Labour and neo-conservatism is therefore one of temperament. Both show a similar attitude towards government, that is activist rather than passive, and which perceives government as being essentially benign, but wishes to achieve outcomes in an indirect manner using aspiration and private interest. It is about using public processes to further private interests, but in a way that is ultimately destructive because the manner in which the processes develop cannot be controlled at the personal level. The crisis is therefore personal, in that it affects particular individuals whose homes have been repossessed, who have lost their jobs or are deep in debt, but which arises out of specific political relations to meeting individual aspiration and a misunderstanding of how government might 'engineer' a commonality of interests.

But there is no real commonality here. The interests of individual households are not the same as those of corporations or government. However, once these elements had all been tied in, there was no possible alternative. The rhetoric of strong government to create free markets could not countenance any conditionality for it to operate, and so the illusion had to be total. Once this illusion began to operate it had to be left to work itself out, because to negate it would be to destroy it. It could not be partial or mitigated. This is because the essence of it was a paradox supporting a series of what were diverse interests at different levels.

The mistake would be to see this as a cynical manipulation or part of some deceit. Rather it was a confluence of interests that became self-supporting and mutually reinforcing: it was where political, financial and micro-economic aspirations came together, and because of the economic and political conditions prevailing at the time, it seemed to work. The elements of electability, profitability and meeting personal ends reinforced and amplified each other and allowed them to develop and be maintained. However, as these three elements were mutually reinforcing, there was no brake or any mechanism that could hold them back and limit the effect of any of them. Rather the three together had an amplifying effect, of enlarging the total and creating a momentum that could not be stopped.

We can see all of this as being entirely rational at the level of the particular actors. Each component part had no incentive to hold back, and so fed the exuberance of the other elements. Households desired cheap credit and financial institutions sought to benefit; government saw owner occupation as popular and tried to create the conditions in which it would blossom.

We might take some liberties with Keynes and suggest that what is at work here is not the paradox of thrift, but a paradox of self-interest. This is where the rational pursuit of self-interest, based on a reasoned and reasonable assumption of the conditions that we were faced with and what was necessary to maintain that situation, actually created the conditions of mutual destruction such that no interests were fully satisfied. This is the reverse situation of that described by Mandeville in his *The Fable of the Bees* (1988),[1] in which our private benefits turn into public vices. This is not because we are stupid or deluded, but because our understanding of the world around us is limited, and we cannot possibly take into account all the factors that come into play when we act in concert with others.

The stupidity, if we can call it that, is the belief that diverse interests can be brought together into some sort of coherent coalition and then consistently controlled. This is the real lesson of housing boom and bust, and we must acknowledge this when we seek to sort it out and try to make sure it does not happen again.

---

1  Mandeville's book is sub-titled *'Private Vices, Publick Benefits'*.

# Chapter 5

# On the virtue of benign neglect

## Introduction

Anarchists used to say about government, 'Don't vote, it only encourages them.' The idea seemed to be that that if you ignored them, they would go away. But government doesn't. People may be put off politics and find the whole business objectionable, but not voting does not mean that the current governments in the US and UK have less power. The situation in these two countries in mid-2009 is, of course, rather different. In the US there is a newly elected president riding a wave of optimism and good will. There is a great sense of possibility and many people, particularly the young, are enthused. In the UK we have a government in its twelfth year, elected in the 2005 general election on the strength of barely a quarter of registered voters and now led by an unelected prime minister who is deeply unpopular. Yet both these governments have legitimacy – they are the government – and they have all the power and control that this legitimacy brings.

The point, therefore, is that ignoring government does not make it go away or make it any less powerful in its ability to influence our lives. What government does matters, whether we acknowledge the fact or not. I have shown in the previous two chapters that government has had a considerable impact on housing and helped to create boom and bust. In response to this we might argue that government should do less, and this indeed will be the basis of my argument, but this still involves government doing something. It is the actor that has to be persuaded to change and to act differently. Put more bluntly, it is something that only government can do.

In this chapter I discuss how we might deal with boom and bust. By that I mean how we can create a situation in which booms and busts are less of a problem for us. I do not argue that we can end the phenomenon of rising and falling housing markets. I believe that we can make things better and that there are clear historical examples which we can draw upon, particularly in recent British history. But there can be no certainty in this, and it would be a very foolish person who claimed that they could solve boom and bust.

The argument I put together here does not contain much in the way of detailed policy mechanisms. I do not suggest new taxes or detailed changes to the planning system; rather, I argue that the problem with housing, or more precisely owner occupation, in the Anglosphere world is one of attitude and culture. In particular, it is about altering the manner in which we view housing and recognising the dual manner in which we tend to operate, whereby housing has both a taken-for-granted existential significance and an economic and financial imperative. My argument is that this duality is out of balance: that we need to take one less for granted and the other less seriously.

My model for this argument is the period in UK housing policy between 1993 and 2003. I would characterise this as a policy of benign neglect towards owner occupation (King 2001). In seeking to recover from a quite considerable recession in housing markets, the Major government steered away from direct intervention in markets and instead placed a priority on stability based on reducing subsidies (the phased withdrawal of mortgage interest tax relief discussed in Chapter 4), continuous high levels of employment and historically low interest rates. This meant that house prices grew steadily in line with earnings and general inflation, but not beyond them. The period of British government in the mid- to late 1990s, when John Major was prime minister, is often characterised as a period of incompetence and sleaze, when the government, which had only a small majority in Parliament, was constantly rocked by small and large scandals. It is often portrayed as a period of little innovation or fresh thinking, when the government was continually caught on the back foot, having to react to issues rather than initiate policy. And of course the electorate seemed to give a particularly uncompromising verdict on the Major government by electing the Labour Party for the first time in 18 years, and with a landslide majority at that.

But it was this very reactive nature of government that was its strength and what allowed it to create stability and security in housing markets. It was precisely the fact that it did not innovate or seek to be radical that was at the heart of its success. In this period the government did not seek to create change, but rather wanted to keep things precisely as they were. It is easy to deride such a policy – and the Major government certainly was, and continues to be, derided – but we need to remember that it was its more radical predecessors and successors that oversaw a boom and bust. It was the Major government that cleared it up and created the conditions, helped no doubt by benign global economic conditions, for over 15 years of continuous economic growth.

We can suggest that the latest housing boom began with the renewed attempt by the Blair government to innovate and create change in the early 2000s, which coincided with a decline in new house building, particularly, but not exclusively, in the social sector (King 2009). The housing green paper (DETR 2000) and the Sustainable Communities Plan (ODPM 2003) saw a renewed interventionism by central government as it sought to plan supply and demand in different parts of the country. Instead of benign neglect, the policy became one of activism and of government knowing best, the results of which we have discussed in the previous chapters.

The emphasis on benign neglect is important because it chimes with our concern for the personal. In placing great store on stability, the Major government provided the opportunity for households to get on with their lives and to use their housing as they saw fit. It was a period when government saw housing as private activity rather than as a national asset. Of course it was not a perfect situation in which no problems existed. There were shortages and there were price increases. It was also a period of cutbacks in social housing expenditure – although not in new building (King 2001) – and of significant rent increases due to the use of private finance. But, in terms of owner occupation, it was a period of stability.

An emphasis on this period is interesting for a further reason. It shows that whilst recessions can have global causes, which no one government can control, let alone the individual households concerned, the solutions might have to be local. What matters is not a new global financial architecture, but the local care of our housing. What is needed is for some body – and this probably has to be national governments – to create the conditions in which we can take care of ourselves. The policies of the 1990s in the UK went some way to achieving this, and so perhaps we need to look again at what is a maligned period to see if we can learn something important.

We are used to being told that we live in an interdependent world, where our livelihoods and life chances are tied to others across the globe. But we can also argue that it was this very sense of interdependence that created the scale of the 2008 recession. In particular, we can point to the idea that risk was being distributed around the world thus creating a more stable system. The idea was that each player would have a lower risk because that risk was being shared. However, this was tested, and found to be false (Cable 2009). Indeed it rested on nothing more than perception; in particular it was perceived that risk was a zero-sum entity, such that sharing meant that each individual held less risk than one person holding it all. But why should this be? As we saw in the Introduction, falling off the bottom of the property ladder is no less painful than coming off the top.

If we use the image of rock climbers who are roped together, we can approximate some sense of this sharing of risk. We may feel more comfortable knowing that there is someone to hold on to us or pull us back if we fall. Yet we also know that if they fall, they can take us with them, indeed they can bring the whole party down. We might feel they can hold us but we are now dependent on them. We start to appreciate that the liability is shared, and the consequence of falling is no less because we are tied to others. We are all bound together and one slip affects us all: in effect, their risk is now mine, and mine is theirs. What has not occurred is a lessening of risk. Indeed, we might even find that the risk is magnified. We might relax and become less conscious of risk and so court disaster and bring others down with us in the process. Safety becomes someone else's problem and we do not have to worry about it.

This sense of interdependency is what was created by government intervention into housing markets in the UK and US. The impression was given that government was providing the support, and so we need not worry. Instead we could enjoy the cold air in our lungs and the spectacular view. In other words, we were able to believe that we could be selfish. We now know that this was a mistake and that being tied together and told we were safe was an illusion. So we need to think of ways of creating independence, of being able to look after ourselves again and to take some responsibility for what is close to us.

The means of achieving this is what this chapter seeks to do. It opens with a consideration of some of the measures taken by governments to deal with the recession. My aim is to show some of the potential consequences of trying to deal with the effects of government action by more government action rather than less. Having done this, I consider a more effective way forward. This begins with a discussion of the concept of affordability and how we need to see this subjectively. My purpose here is to give the issue of personal responsibility some context. This leads to a discussion on the distinction between markets and owner occupation, between the process of providing certain goods and those goods themselves. My aim is to show the instrumentality of markets and hence give proper emphasis to dwellings rather than the means of provision. The final section of this chapter deals with the issue of benign neglect and how this might be a suitable means of mitigating some of the effects of boom and bust.

## What can governments do?

The discussion on free markets and capitalism since 2008 has tended towards hyperbole. Perhaps this was not surprising in the rather febrile atmosphere immediately after the collapse of Lehman Brothers and the public scandals about bankers' salaries and bonuses. However, the language used by politicians and commentators has not always been helpful or even particularly enlightening. In particular, much of the debate seemed to be predicated on the assumption that the world consisted of virtually unlimited markets and very low levels of government intervention. There has been talk of 'market fundamentalism', and calls for a return to a more balanced assessment of the role of government. This seemed to be based on the argument that there had been a return to some sort of Victorian laissez-faire in which government has withdrawn almost entirely. However, as we have stated, the activities of governments in the UK and US have hardly been minimal. The US government takes over 30 per cent of GDP and the UK government consistently over 40 per cent. The Anglo-Saxon model is hardly light on regulation and intervention, even when compared to Europe. Indeed intervention is much higher than in China, which still has minimal social protection. The actual difference in terms of regulation and intervention between, say, France and the US is rather small, being a question of degree rather than of fundamentals, and the difference between the UK and other European countries is even less marked.

Perhaps what is more important here is the difference in mentality and rhetoric towards markets. It is about how different critics perceive capitalism and its role in the crisis and therefore what role is seen for government in the present and the future. It is interesting that the critics of market fundamentalism and those calling for more government regulation, particularly in Germany, are also those who are most resistant to calls from the US for more financial stimulus from government. The governments of Bush and Obama have been more activist than many in continental Europe, despite the rhetoric of the latter being more pro-government. Indeed, as we have seen, the US government's intervention in housing markets has been both long-term and considerable.

Likewise, the New Labour government was very far from minimalist in its interventions. It has been extremely centralising in its actions and has extended regulation considerably. It might have spoken of light-touch regulation, but, as we saw in Chapters 3 and 4, this has applied only in certain selected areas and not to civil liberties, welfare, education, health or housing policy.

In terms of dealing with the housing recession the main approach taken by government has been to try to return to the situation prior to 2007. The Brown government sought to encourage or force banks and building societies to return to the levels of lending at the height of the boom. Alongside this the Bank of England, in common with other central banks across the world, reduced interest rates dramatically, and the government then called on lenders to reduce their mortgage rates accordingly. However, at the same time the government insisted that those financial institutions it had bailed out should make a reasonable rate of return so they could pay off their liabilities to government.

The belief, early in the recession, was that the priority for government was to reflate housing markets and engineer a quick return to positive house price inflation. This would provide security to households and bring back the feel-good factor. It would encourage people to buy and sell dwellings, and lenders would be prepared to offer reasonable terms in the expectation of increasing values relative to mortgage debt. Similarly house price inflation would encourage developers to start building again as they sold down their inventories. And, of course, politicians would benefit from the upswing in confidence. Appreciating house prices will, in the main, deal with the problems of negative equity, the situation in which households owe more than the value of their property. The priority in 2008 was therefore to try to bolster confidence and use interest rates to turn around the market. The UK government also sought to stimulate the market by increasing the threshold on stamp duty from £125,000 to £175,000 in the hope that this would stimulate activity in the market.

However, the emphasis later in 2008 and into 2009 shifted away from trying to reflate the market towards interventions aimed at preventing mortgage repossession or foreclosure. Government sought to do this through mortgage protection schemes and by putting pressure on lenders to be more lenient in their dealings with indebted households. In the US, President

Obama introduced a $75 billion package aimed at dealing with foreclosures (Ward 2009). Funding would be made available to lenders to allow them to reduce mortgage rates to lenders. In addition, fresh capital was provided for Fannie Mae and Freddie Mac to help them refinance mortgages. The aim of this intervention was to reduce the monthly mortgage payments of up to 9 million households in danger of foreclosure. Government, however, is not providing all the cost of this reduction, with lenders themselves being expected to contribute. Policies in the UK have been much more limited with £1 billion being made available for mortgage rescue schemes.

We can speculate on what effect these sorts of policies might have and whether they are justified. Clearly, if the aim is to reduce repossessions, then they will have done their job. But this assumes that these schemes are the most effective means of doing so and that they do not have any other effects. For example, if a qualifying threshold is applied, then this may encourage people to cause their situation to worsen in order to qualify for government aid. There may then be the potential for moral hazard where government action actually increases the incidence of what it is trying to prevent. We might also argue that these schemes penalise those who continue with their payments, especially when lenders have to bear some of the costs of reducing payments themselves and seek to recoup them elsewhere.

These schemes prevent lenders from taking the appropriate action to protect their interests and might make them reluctant to lend to certain riskier groups in the future if they feel that government will interfere with the contractual arrangements they have made with customers. They impinge on property rights and legitimate interests founded on contractual arrangements. In addition, lenders are not able to liquidate their assets as they see fit, and funds, therefore, remain tied up in a loss making situation. These schemes will also prevent markets from working properly by reducing the flow of available dwellings, particularly at the bottom end of markets.

There is an assumption underpinning these schemes that the behaviour of borrowers is legitimate and worthy of support, whilst the lenders have somehow acted illegitimately. Government might try mitigating this by seeking to limit the scheme only to 'responsible' or 'hard working' households, and not to those who have acted 'irresponsibly'. Yet these judgements are hard to establish and might well be arbitrary and impossible to determine in practice. Of course from the point of view of the lender who is owed the money, what does it matter how the debt has accrued?

Another point often raised in discussing how to deal with the recession is to see it as an opportunity to rebalance or transform housing, either by building social dwellings (Pickard 2009) or through a major transformation of mortgage finance. The argument seems to be that this is a once-in-a-generation opportunity to change fundamentally housing markets and the manner in which houses are bought and sold. However, we can question just what constituency there is for radical change. Why would politicians and the general public accept or even seek such major changes when they are already experiencing a major dislocation caused by falling house prices, a decline in mortgage finance, increased risk of unemployment, and so on? As we have seen, the main incentives appear to be to return to the situation that obtained prior to 2007.

This attitude is precisely the problem, and some sort of change is required. However, I argue that what is needed is not a root and branch reform of housing finance, but a change in attitude towards housing and finance and how they are seemingly inseparably joined together. We need to alter the manner in which we have come to relate to our housing and how we perceive it. We need to downgrade our perception of housing as an asset and see it more as a store of memory and a place of comfort and security. But this is very difficult to achieve. It is not obviously dealt with by policy prescriptions, but rather concerns how we view our dwelling as an object. In the rest of this chapter I explore how this might be achieved.

## What can I afford?

One of the most abused words in housing policy over the last decade – and there have been many (King 2004, 2006) – is 'affordability'. Of course the concept has always been important in housing policy, but it has now taken on a particular meaning whereby it denotes only low-income housing. As a result we now hear planners and housing professionals earnestly talking about the number of dwellings (in fact they would say 'homes') being built in an area of which a certain percentage of them will be 'affordable'. This is clearly a nonsensical idea, in that it is absurd that any developer would build unaffordable housing. The term now tends to be used as a means of allowing government to place low-cost home ownership schemes at the same level in its policy-making as social housing. The term is used to suggest that the housing is affordable to everyone, including those on low incomes. But using the word in this way means it takes on a moral dimension, in that housing that is not designated 'affordable' is somehow suspect and improper. However, the opposite of affordable housing is not that which is unaffordable, but that which can only be afforded by some. Ironically, of course, these households are more likely to be able to comfortably afford their housing than those in so called 'affordable housing'.

But, assuming that we allow people any degree of choice over where and in what they live, there will always be some housing that will be too expensive for some households and therefore be unaffordable. As Sowell (2007) has argued, there is a tendency to see unaffordability as somehow unfair, when actually it is just the result of supply and demand based on conditions of scarcity. It is neither moral, nor necessarily unfair, rather simply a situation of there not being enough housing of a particular type. In the UK we tend to argue that in this situation there is unmet housing need when in fact it is merely a mismatch of supply and demand, and a belief that households have a right to the sort of housing they want rather than having to make do with alternatives that they can actually afford. We assume that because people want to live in London and the south-east of England they should be able to and that housing should be sufficiently affordable to allow them to do so. We have considered this issue in some detail in Chapter 2 and suggested that whilst people can clearly choose to live where they like, their decisions will have consequences in terms of quality of life, as well as affordability.

Mentioning the situation in London brings us to the very real paradox with regard to affordability: the areas where affordability is deemed to be at its worst are also the areas of highest demand. There are very few empty dwellings here, even though people supposedly cannot afford to live in them. This clarifies what the debate on affordability is actually about. Affordability, we might say, does not affect demand and nor does it increase supply, in the short term at least. Housing in London is affordable, but what matters is who can afford it and what happens to those who cannot. In practical terms, most people can afford something. Households may be paying more than they would like, or are not living in an area they would choose, or are not able to have the sort of dwelling they might prefer. But they can afford what they have.

This being so, why should we feel that all housing should be affordable to everyone? If housing is scarce, then should we not accept this as a fact of life and that the market is best at allocating what is available. In a country such as the UK or the US it is often not the case that the housing does not exist, but rather that not everyone is able to afford the sort of housing they want, where they want it. The most effective means of dealing with this problem is to allow the market to react and build more housing, or for consumers to make alternative plans.

The use of affordability in housing policy makes sense only if we turn the word into a pseudo-technical term. Housing becomes, therefore, either 'affordable' or not. The concept comes to be seen as an absolute when, in fact, it is anything but; rather affordability is properly based on a number of objective and subjective factors. These include the amount that we would ideally wish to pay, and the amount that we actually can pay, which may well be different from the amount we would like to, in that we might have to sacrifice some areas of expenditure (entertaining, holidays, a new car) in order to fund our housing. It is determined by what sort of dwelling we want and whether it is available at the right price. This in turn depends on how flexible we are, which is determined not only by our preferences, but also by our family circumstances, employment, how long we feel we can wait, and so on. Clearly, what helps or hinders this decision-making is what alternatives exist and whether we have a realistic and accurate understanding of our position relative to housing markets. Indeed the state of housing markets is an important factor with regard to affordability, obviously in terms of prices, but also in the level of activity and whether it is consistent across all markets. Markets work only if there are sellers as well as buyers and so our actions are determined in part by the choices made by others. We also need to factor in the availability of alternative forms of provision by public and private bodies.

Our decision-making is also affected by our view of the future in terms of our personal prospects and what we think will happen in the economy as a whole. Do we feel we shall be better or worse off in a year's time? Will we still have a job? Are prices going up or down and how quickly? Will it change? What about the impact of interest rates? Is government policy going to change? All these questions impact on our considerations of what is affordable and show the huge complexity of the issues around the affordability of housing. Some of these factors are subjective and others objective. We can change some, whilst others we cannot, and some are easier to control than others. An arbitrary definition based on average earnings might help academic debate, but it cannot capture the very real nuances of the actual decision-making processes used by households. Some people are prepared to pay more than the average and can afford to do so comfortably, whilst others could afford to do likewise but choose not to because their priorities are elsewhere. As we saw in Chapter 2, some people live in more expensive areas because of the nature of their work, because of family connections or because they like the area and local community, whilst others are prepared to commute so that they can afford a more relaxed lifestyle for their families. The real danger is that we ignore these subjective choices, apply a purely arbitrary test of affordability to complex behaviours and market conditions and so skew the market by helping certain groups, such as designated key workers like nurses and police officers, whilst harming other low- and middle-income workers not seen as 'key', such as taxi-drivers and office workers.

Of course just because much of this decision-making is subjective, it does not imply that there are no constraints. For most households the decision on what they can afford is hedged around by what is available, at what price and by what financial institutions are prepared to lend to us. In addition, the flexibility that exists within markets might not be matched by the flexibility of our incomes and lifestyles. If housing becomes scarce and prices rise, then housing becomes less affordable. If this is a permanent change, then our measure of affordability must also alter, at least in the informal sense of what we are prepared to commit, knowing the only alternative is not to buy. We might suggest that the decision-making process for most people is reactive, in that most will have a restricted income which tends to be static or rises only slowly.

This suggests that the idea of affordability is very much tied up with our own experience and expectations of housing rather than it being determined purely by objective or external factors. What matters is our perception of housing markets based on our need or desire to enter them. For most of us, most of the time, affordability is not an issue. We have made a decision about where to live, and it is settled. Assuming that our circumstances do not change, then affordability is something we can take for granted.

The problem with thinking on affordability, therefore, is that it is taken to be a thing in itself rather than merely instrumental to our subjective condition. Affordable housing is taken to be a thing, an object, when it is really understandable only as a relation. Every time someone uses the term 'affordable housing', we should ask them, 'Affordable for whom?'

## Markets and housing

This sense of the instrumental nature of things brings us back to markets and what they are for. Housing markets and housing are not the same thing, any more than apples and fruit and vegetable stalls are one and the same. We need to distinguish between the getting and the using; the good and its means of delivery. Of course there is a link between them: we buy things because of their utility and this may heighten and lessen over time. If markets do not work well, this may lessen our ability to access them. But, still, markets are not the same as the goods themselves: rather one depends upon the other. The good has a primary relation with us, which in the case of housing might be permanent. The market is merely derivative and temporary: our access depends on the need or desire to acquire the good and once we have it, we can withdraw from the market. Sometimes, our involvement with markets is regular, whilst for other goods we engage with them only infrequently.

The problem is that we might concentrate on the market instead of the good. This is where we focus on housing in terms of finance, and buying and selling. But it is the placing of these derived markets over the thing being traded and sought after that causes the difficulties for us. We need to buy and sell, but not for their sake. We generally welcome a sophisticated market for housing as it allows us to buy and sell, and gain the finance we need to achieve this. But we do not want this to be the driver or the key element in the process. We want markets to remain in their place. It is an organising mechanism, which may be particularly effective, but still it has its limits.

Clearly we would find it difficult to operate without markets. They are the best means for achieving our wants. Accordingly, we tend to be suspicious of those who question markets. Partly this is because of the opportunism involved, and partly it is because we ask ourselves how we live and so what do others do. Just where do they get things from? But also we are suspicious because we know that housing provided by markets offers greater choice, more options and freedom (and more responsibility) than if it were provided by the state. The fact that the majority of housing in most developed countries is provided through markets is not coincidence, but is rather a signal that this is the way it works best (King 2003).

Perhaps one of the benefits, if we can use such a term, of the housing recession is to show just how dependent we are on markets for our housing, and just what limited possibilities there are for any alternatives. Of course we might say that we should not start from here, from this position of apparent dependence on markets in which 70 per cent of households are owners. Instead we should take this opportunity to rethink housing policy and the dominance of owner occupation. But, as we have discussed above, just how likely is this to actually happen, outside universities and certain think-tanks? On what basis could we achieve the sorts of change needed to ensure a system that is no longer so reliant on just one tenure? Either we must have mass confiscation of private property, a truly massive building programme of literally millions of houses, or some other mechanism whereby private dwellings are sold to either private or social landlords. As we considered in Chapter 4, this presumes access to huge amounts of private and public funding, as well as the political will and a willingness of households currently in owner occupation to live in alternative tenures. But most households are not clamouring for social or private renting. Rather they want to be able to afford their mortgage; they hope that their dwelling increases in value and that they might be able to offer some security to their children. Most of the time in the US and UK this is achievable through owner occupation, and this is not because people are deluded or suffer from the effects of hegemonic discourses or whatever, but because it is rational for them to expect it under current and established conditions. It readily appears to be beneficial and achievable for most people, most of the time. What benefit would there be for them in accepting any major change from what they have become used to? Moreover, why would we expect politicians to propose these changes? What would be the electoral benefits of doing so? It is interesting that there has been very little attempt by politicians in either the UK or US to question the role of owner occupation or seek to replace it with any other tenure. At the margins there are those calling for more social housing and for a shift in emphasis, but this is not making any headway in government. Indeed, as we have discussed above, the emphasis has been to ensure that we return to steadily increasing house prices as quickly and painlessly as we can.

And whilst we might argue that these arguments are not particularly principled, but rather based on the ready acceptance of the status quo, we also need to appreciate that whilst practicality and popularity might not provide overwhelming or even sufficient arguments in favour of a policy or practice, they do matter and cannot be ignored. Those seeking to change housing policy have to deal with the fact that they are dealing with what most people have, and expect to have, to the extent that they take it for granted. Any change will therefore be very difficult to impose. And 'impose' is indeed the word: it is unlikely to be taken up voluntarily.

The way we act in markets is important, and this needs to be remembered when we talk of crises. In the discussion on affordability above we questioned the nature of housing need and suggested that much of what we refer to as housing need is actually discretionary, in that it relates to moves we wish to make and which are based on choice rather than any imperative. We choose to seek a bigger house or to move jobs or downsize because the children have left and so on. In most cases our needs are created by the choices we have made: need is instrumental to our choices (King 2003). This does not mean that we should not seek to achieve our ends if we can. If people can afford to move, and want to, and if it harms no one else unduly in the process, then there is no reason to stop it or argue against it. And it is precisely this that markets are best at achieving.

This idea of much housing market activity being discretionary puts a rather different gloss onto the idea of housing need and markets. Much of the fall in activity in the housing market, and the consequent fall in house prices, is not therefore fatal, but is rather merely hampering discretionary activity. When it might be problematic, of course, is that not all activity is discretionary and some is doubtless borne out of genuine need. It may well be that it is this non-discretionary part of the market that is most hampered.

However, in mitigation, the effect of falling house prices is to make housing much more affordable to those in need, provided they are able to get a reasonable mortgage offer or are able to wait out the recession. The market in a recession is moving in a way that is favourable to this group of buyers. Whilst this might be a hard argument to sell in a recession, it does need to be stated clearly that falling house prices benefit precisely those groups currently most excluded from the market. So provided they are able to wait, they will then find themselves in a much stronger position once mortgage finance becomes available.

Much of the discussion on housing policy in England since 2000 has been over affordability and access (CLG 2007; HM Treasury 2004; ODPM 2003). The aim has been to try to create more affordable housing and increase supply generally. But no remedies were developed that had anything but a marginal impact, such as an increase in building (which proved short-lived due to the recession), or were relatively unpopular, like Key Worker Living or HomeBuy. Might we not argue that the recession has largely dealt with the affordability problem? Markets have, so to speak, corrected the imbalance that had built up between supply and demand. This does not mean it has been comfortable for anyone and that there were no casualties, but this is what markets do, and it will, we might say, prove to be rather more effective than any prescriptions that government has managed.

This does not mean that government has no role; however, this role is somewhat different from that which government expects to play. If most people remain well housed; if much of our market activity is discretionary; and if markets are moving in a direction that is favourable to those who are most excluded, then what government has to do is not intervene massively and seek to transform housing markets and owner occupation. Rather government needs to remember that markets are means and not ends in themselves, and that what it should seek to do is ensure that we are able to use our dwellings just as we please. It can achieve this best by following, what I term, a policy of benign neglect.

## Benign neglect

When the recession is over, what do we want? We might see the answer as obvious – a functioning owner-occupied sector – and to an extent that is correct. But is that enough? Would, and should, we be happy to go back to where we were before 2007, or should we seek something that has been refined and changed to prevent future crises?

Of course choosing to retain a strong owner-occupied sector does not mean that we would necessarily return to the situation that immediately preceded 2007, in which housing markets and regulators were complacent, in which there was too much emphasis on dwelling as a material asset, and in which the priority for government was maintaining the buoyancy of the market and the attendant feel-good factor. On one level there is little wrong with this: feeling secure and comfortable is surely something to be welcomed. But in the light of the recession was this complacency based on anything secure or was it an illusion?

For most people, most of the time, their attitude towards their housing was certainly not based on any illusion. They definitively were secure – and many remain so – and their dwelling functioned as it should. They were, and are, financially secure and can sustain their dwelling and their lifestyle. If we view our position relatively, as we may well tend to do, we might feel less secure now than in the past and we might remain cautious for a considerable period of time. But, in absolute terms, how we live is sustainable.

The hardest thing to argue in a recession is that housing markets, generally speaking, work well. In normal times housing markets seem benign and helpful to us, giving us greater freedom to choose how we want to live. However, we have learnt in Chapters 3 and 4 that markets are often not left to work as they should. Markets are not left to operate in a free way, and perhaps they never have been. In a modern economy we cannot extricate the workings of markets from the actions of government. This suggests, therefore, that we seek a relationship between government and markets that allows us to maximise the use and meaning we are able to draw from our housing.

Many of the proposals that have come from government, including those considered briefly above, have involved more intervention and regulation. This is based on the premise that markets have failed and so need to be more tightly controlled. But what if, instead of greater regulation, we try the opposite and free housing from as much government intervention as possible? In particular, there is the problem of encouraging ownership at the margins, which we have seen consistently in the US and in the UK since the 1970s. This sought to draw ever larger numbers of low-income households into owner occupation and so created financial products which led to huge instabilities in global markets.

A more sustainable situation would be to return to the benign neglect pursued by the Major government in the UK in the mid-1990s. This saw government taking a rather minimalist position towards housing and not really seeking to actively encourage owner occupation with any special measures. The Major government had to respond to the housing boom and bust of the late 1980s and early 1990s. Initially it introduced a number of measures including mortgage rescue schemes and the so called Housing Market Package in 1992 with the aim of buying up empty and unsold properties (King 1996). The impact of this form of intervention was minimal and was soon ended when Kenneth Clarke became Chancellor of the Exchequer in 1993. He took the view that the Housing Market Package had been a waste of money which had merely benefited private developers rather than individual households in danger of repossession (King 2001). A further reason for the change in policy was a broadening understanding of the embedded nature of owner occupation in the wider economy. The Major government appeared to grasp that what mattered most was not government supports, such as tax relief, but secure employment prospects, stable interest rates and low inflation. The housing market needed economic stability from government so that house prices did not rise too quickly and mortgage rates were stable and affordable. Hence, as we have seen, the Major government began the process of phasing out tax relief in 1994/5.

This policy was maintained by the New Labour government elected in 1997. It continued to phase out MITR and abolished it completely in 2000. Moreover, it appeared to concur with Clarke's view on the need for stability. The 2000 housing green paper stated:

> The main contribution to government can make to sustainable homeownership is a robust economy in all parts of the country and a strong system of consumer protection. As a

result of our economic policies, homeowners are benefiting from relatively low mortgage interest rates and rising living standards. . . . We are determined to avoid a return to the boom and bust economy of the past, which eroded the security many expected from their homes and created an uncertain climate for one of the most important long-term financial commitments which most people make.

(DETR 2000: 30)

So the initial view of New Labour, in its determination to avoid boom and bust, was that stability was to be preferred rather than specific and targeted interventions. As we have seen, this policy did not last and the years after 2000 saw a more activist approach to owner occupation, with government seeking to attract new owners into the tenure and ensure that markets remained buoyant.

The key problem for government in this position – and neither the Major government nor New Labour would admit this openly – is that the policy of stability implies that there are practical limits to the growth of owner occupation. If government takes the view that its role is to maintain benign conditions for owner occupation but not to encourage it, then it follows that the tenure will not necessarily grow, or rather that any growth will be naturally based on market conditions and the real costs of housing rather than any prompting from government. This, in turn, will have a beneficial effect on other tenures, in that it will legitimise them. There will still be the problem of 'second best', and this is something that we cannot yet really avoid, in that we cannot wish away history and the manner in which ownership has been viewed and supported over the last generation. But recognising a limit to ownership, in the sense of not pushing it further, will create a degree of stability in all tenures.

Government can seek to create stability through a number of means, including consistently low and stable interest rates, low inflation and consistently high levels of employment. In addition, government should seek to avoid complex interventions in the market and make it a matter of policy that it will not, as a general rule, intervene to encourage or manage the tenure. This has implications for the planning system, and government should move to a more liberal planning regime that contains local incentives to build and allows decisions to be made locally (Leunig 2007). Leunig proposes that planning should be localised and based on the creation of local markets for land use and decided democratically. Such a position extricates planning from the interest of central government and frees up local communities to determine the level of development they desire.

We should note from this list of measures that none of them relates to the structure of owner occupation as such; they are actually external to the tenure. They allow the tenure to operate and for households to take decisions but without seeking to manage the tenure itself or alter the incentive structures of households. This is a crucially important point, which relates back to the discussion about the difference between housing and housing markets: sustainable and viable support for owner occupation needs to take the form of a framework for individual decision-making and not the creation of particular structures. Government can certainly provide what might be termed 'artificial' incentives through intervention, but these are seldom sustainable. In addition, the scale of specific government interventions can seldom match the effects of the other factors, such as employment and inflation, as we see every time there is a recession.

The aim of government should be one of neutrality and to refrain from the promotion of one form of tenure, no matter how popular. Instead government should let tenures grow organically according to market conditions. The key reason for this is that no part of the economy is structurally independent of the rest. We should not assume that one sector, such as owner occupation or financial services, can expand rapidly without expecting there to be spill-over effects. Housing is embedded in the economy in many ways: it is built by private companies; funding is obtained from commercial lenders, who in turn need to ensure a source of funds from somewhere; households pay for their housing from their own income and they need to ensure that this is maintained via the labour market, and so on. Also, as pointed out in Chapter 4, government needs to remember that corporatism is not the same as capitalism and that large corporations have little interest in maintaining free and open markets.

Owner occupation works because of what it lets us do, because of what it allows us to sustain. This is a form of life that builds from the inside outwards. The crucial supports for dwelling are internal and not external. They are really private and depend on the relationship we, as self-directed individuals, have with the dwelling itself. But these internal supports do need care and close attention, just as those we live with rely on us for support until they can become independent and sustain themselves.

Some households cannot manage this internal structure and the responsibilities it brings. This has nothing to do with discrimination, inequality or injustice, but rather is a matter of capability and circumstance. We should not push and bend the tenure so that it is made to fit those who would otherwise struggle and fail. We should realise that owner occupation is not for everyone. This does not involve placing restrictions on the tenure, but rather just standing back and allowing those who can to prosper and those who cannot to pursue other alternatives.

What determines whether ownership is possible and tenable is the ability of the household to access housing markets and sustain themselves as a result. We should listen to the signals that the market is giving us. This is not because markets are omniscient: they do not have feelings or intelligence of their own. Markets, however, have a hardness, an implacability, so that they can be unforgiving. They are not capable of making allowances for the special case. This is why they work so well, but also why they may not suit us all. This means that, for some, the means of gaining knowledge is through their own failure. However, for others it is the very difficulty of accessing the market itself. Most of us are quick to realise that things are too precarious when we have to stretch too far.

In particular, government needs to recognise this. In the past politicians have sought to support owner occupation and proffer the view that it is suitable for all. But this is akin to redefining swimming to include keeping your feet on the bottom. This might give us the illusion we are swimming, and others at a distance might be conned by it as well. But we can only carry the illusion in the shallows, where it is safe. If we go out of our depth, then we realise what swimming really involves; we are unprepared and there may not be anyone around to help us out. Government intervention means we are being kept artificially safe and remain unprepared, and no matter how convincingly government tells us otherwise, we are deluding ourselves if we believe it. Moreover, most people know that when their feet are on the ground, they are not really swimming: they know that they are not being honest.

We also know that government is not capable of preventing the big wave from coming and knocking us over. It is as ineffectual as any other agency and individual in holding back the tide. It can try to clear up the mess and organise a rescue, but this is palliative and not preventative. This might lead us towards fatalism, and to the view that there is little that can be done. We have no option but to live at the mercy of the market. Is there really nothing we can do? In the short-to-medium term the answer is probably a qualified 'no'. There are simply no incentives or opportunities to allow this. Our only prospect is to learn to swim, and then to remain cautious at all times. We should not go beyond what we think is safe and perhaps we should build in a margin of safety: ultimately it is up to us to make sure that we are safe.

However, things do and will change. They just do so in ways that we are not always able to pre-empt and plan for in advance. This means that the next recession will be quite different from the last one, and so any measures we might take in response to this one could be ineffective. Indeed, as with the US Federal Reserve's response to the dotcom bust in 2000, the actions we take might actually create the next boom and bust (Shiller 2008). Government action always has unintended consequences and this can never be avoided.

But the main reason we need not be fatalistic is that most of us, most of the time, are well housed. And there is no real reason to assume that this will change. This is not complacency, but a plain fact. We should not use this as an excuse to avoid helping those who are not well housed or who cannot maintain themselves. But nor should we forget just what our housing allows us to do. It allows us to do what we wish to do, to live and set our aims without the conscious concern of daily subsistence. This is what we ought to focus on: not the value of the dwelling, but its qualities and what it does for us in all its fullness, its physicality and its enclosure. We should remember and relish its ability to act as a store, not of wealth, but of memories and of care. Housing, to reiterate, is not the same as finance.

# Conclusions
## A plea for sanity

There is a natural tendency to see the issue of boom and bust simply in terms of finance and economics. With regard to housing, this means we see our dwellings in terms of their economic value, and we focus on our housing costs. We see housing as property, as something with a value. Perhaps it is inevitable that we do this: in a boom the values are increasing and we might feel wealthier; in a bust we might feel we are losing money.

But, in doing so, we can lose sight of the fact that our dwelling still works for us as a nest, a shelter and a refuge. Perhaps one outcome we should seek from the post-2007 recession is to break the connection between housing and finance, or rather not to see housing just in financial terms, and I speak here as an academic who teaches and writes on housing finance. What I mean by this is that we should start to appreciate how we can use our dwelling and what it means to go beyond the financial; that when we put the bills and the calculator away, we can relax, be comfortable and share our quiet privacy with those we love. We need to remember that stability and stasis are the ultimate means of freedom from boom and bust.

I can remember a decade or so ago making a point in a presentation I was giving in a seminar on housing and markets that what was needed was to separate housing from the economy. I felt that I knew what I intended by this. But a Dutch academic, with scrupulous politeness, asked me what I meant by this because he said that he just could not see what this would involve: how can we separate housing from the economy? I think

I mumbled some answer about the difference between economic and human values, but I did not feel that I had answered the question well, and said as much when we retired to the pub a bit later. I had to admit that whilst it felt like a good idea, how it might actually be achieved left me silent.

A lot of the work I have done over the last decade has been concerned with trying to make sense of this statement. I was convinced then, and still am now, that housing is not just about economics or even finance; or rather it need not be. There is a lot more to housing than money: it is important, but it is not everything. So now, after a lot of work, what do I mean? In essence, what I think I mean now is that we have to be clear about the meaning of housing; that what matters is how we use housing and how this generates significance for us. Housing is for living in and this trumps issues of costs and value. Meaning and use are sufficient in themselves, but costs and value are question-begging. The use of our dwelling needs no further justification, but the money we spend on it does.

This answer does not fully succeed in separating housing from the economy. Indeed it is probably not possible to do so, especially in a society based on markets and choice. I would even venture to say that we would not want to separate them totally. However, seeing meaning as distinct from the money does help us, in that it tells us what really matters about our housing.

So no matter what the state of the economy is, we can still use our housing. Its instrumental quality does not alter just because it is worth more or less than last year. And of crucial importance to us is the fact that we can use our dwelling to help us hide from the worst of the recession, so that when the storm clouds roll over us we can lock up, hunker down and wait for the storm to clear.

It is this very distinction that makes the concept of really private finance so important. The essence of really private finance is that it focuses on how we maintain ourselves and those things close to us. It therefore focuses on the instrumental quality of finance and makes it subservient to the meanings we place on our housing. The finance helps us keep things close: it is a means to provide and maintain what is perhaps our most important resource.

Really private finance allows us to see the links between finance and use, and how our interests and aims are connected to the wider world. This connection is a subjective one, which, so to speak, goes from in to out. It is mediated by the meanings we place on what is around us. Clearly we can be seriously affected by what is outside, by what is not close to us. At some time the outside will impinge upon us, and this will alter the way in which we behave. Yet the basic mechanisms of decision-making, and the place where we make those decisions, do not change. The conditions we operate within may alter: at some times the constraints will be greater, but the process by which we operate remains the same. We still act in the same manner regardless of the pressure which we face. This is crucial, in that it forces us back to the personal, to the actual impact on us of choice.

So, to state the obvious, houses are for living in, and this is how we should see housing boom and bust. They are not just assets or investments, and neither are they ever just liabilities. They are the bricks and mortar that offer us physical protection. They keep us dry, warm and safe, and they are stores of memory, receptacles of our relationships, the base for our intimacies, our personal gains and losses.

Most people want to know if boom and bust can be avoided. Clearly this is what we would like to be able to achieve, and it is what politicians find themselves having to promise. But we have to admit that it probably cannot be prevented. However, the scale of these ups and downs can be moderated, so that the highs and lows are not so extreme. As I have argued in Chapter 5, the way to achieve this is not through action, but through neglect, through doing nothing. Ronald Reagan said about government: 'Don't just do something, stand there!' This is the model that we should work towards, because government action has itself caused major problems and magnified boom and bust.

There really can be no certainty in this. There is no possible way in which we can predict the future of housing markets and how they will be affected by other parts of the economy. This is one reason for trying to insulate our housing, but it can never be completely successful. What we can say, however, is that attempts to control markets and to meet certain policy aims have failed, and failed badly, and this is despite the best of intentions and a lot of research.

For most people, most of the time, housing markets work quite well. It is at the margins where there are problems, and this is due in large part to the actions of government in promoting owner occupation as widely as it has. Of course this policy worked well with the Right to Buy, but only because of the policy's simplicity and the clear incentives offered by government. Because of this it would be difficult to replicate the policy, and we should not necessarily expect it to be repeated. Indeed, there has been no public policy that has even come close to its success over the last 30 years (King 2010). Consumers of the Right to Buy were protected by the nature of the policy – it provided them with a subsidised asset which was also their established home – whilst those on low incomes who bought on the open market from sub-prime lenders were not supported by anything but their own resources and wits. The Right to Buy provided a one-off support and then left households to deal with their own lives from then onwards. They needed no further intervention from this point onwards. In this sense we can see it as a form of government intervention that was genuinely liberating. But this is a very rare thing in public policy, and seldom have any other policies reached this level of response.

We could say that the lesson to draw from this is for government to try harder, to come up with a policy with the same capacity as the Right to Buy. Government should learn from the Right to Buy and get it right again. But, equally, we might take the view that it is so hard to get it right that government ought not to intervene. If failure is so likely, why not just accept that government cannot do that much? This is indeed the key lesson to learn from the Right to Buy: it is so very hard to get the policy-making right, and we need to be very lucky in order to get just the correct sort of mechanisms, circumstances and capable households together in the one place at the right time to make a policy work well. The likelihood of this happening with any frequency is doubtful in the extreme, and we should not make the mistake of trying to force the situation and make the situation fit the policy.

The key issue for government must be that it does no harm. It must not try to do what it cannot achieve. This means, of course, as a first step, being very clear just what it is that government can do. The basis of government action should be to ensure individuals can use their ability to take decisions and that they carry the consequences of these decisions.

The conclusion we have to reach, therefore, is that government should do less rather than more. We should get government to sit back and do only what it can do well without seeking to encourage any one tenure, however laudable its aims might be and regardless of popularity. This involves admitting, as many on both the left and the right of politics are seemingly loath to do, that owner occupation might not be for everyone and that there is a limit to how far it can grow. This limit is not an immutable one, and we should not expect to be able to predict exactly where the level will be in the future. Indeed we do not need to set a limit ourselves – this would be arbitrary and unreasonable – but instead we should let markets decide where that limit is on the basis of what households can afford and what seems right for local communities. This will differ over time and from place to place, but what is wrong with that?

In response to this, some might argue that many households lack sufficient financial knowledge and have taken poor decisions. But in response to this we need to suggest that buying a house with a mortgage is hardly a perverse decision to have taken. The problem is rather with the manner in which housing markets have been regulated and the resulting structures devised by financial institutions which sought maximum profitability by generating and then transferring risk. It is an error to see the problem with owner occupation itself. The fault is with government policy for encouraging the tenure beyond its natural bounds and enabling financial institutions to cash in on this. This suggests it is not an issue of regulating owner occupation, but reducing the influence of government.

What is needed, then, is some simple sanity, some plain thinking and humility about what it is that we can do about markets, and then leave them, and those who use them, be.

# Bibliography

Akerlof, G. and Shiller, R. (2009), *Animal Spirits: How Human Psychology Drives the Economy, and Why It Matters for Global Capitalism*, Princeton, NJ, Princeton University Press.

Birch, J. (2009), 'No Access', *ROOF*, 34, 3, May/June, pp. 18–21.

Blair, T. (1998), *The Third Way: New Politics for the New Century*, London, Fabian Society.

Boddy, M. (1992), 'From Mutual Interests to Market Forces', in Grant, C. (ed.), *Built to Last?: Reflections on British Housing Policy*, London, ROOF, pp. 40–9.

Booth, P. (ed.) (2009), *Verdict on the Crash: Causes and Policy Implications*, London, Institute of Economic Affairs.

Brown, T. (1999), 'The Third Way', in Brown, T. (ed.), *Stakeholder Housing: A Third Way*, London, Pluto Press, pp. 8–32.

Brummer, A. (2008), *The Crunch: The Scandal of Northern Rock and the Escalating Credit Crisis*, London, Random House.

Bryant, W. and Zick, C. (2006), *The Economic Organisation of the Household*, 2nd edn, Cambridge, Cambridge University Press.

Butler, E. (2009), 'The Financial Crisis: Blame Governments, Not Bankers', in Booth, P. (ed.) *Verdict on the Crash: Causes and Policy Implications*, London, Institute of Economic Affairs, pp. 51–8.

Cable, V. (2009), *The Storm: The World Economic Crisis and What It Means*, London, Atlantic Books.

Clapham, D. (2005), *The Meaning of Housing: A Pathways Approach*, Bristol, Policy Press.

Cohan, W. (2009), *House of Cards: How Wall Street's Gamblers Broke Capitalism*, London, Allen Lane.

Communities and Local Government (CLG) (2007), *Homes for the Future: More Affordable, More Sustainable*, London, The Stationery Office.

Congdon, T. (2009), *Central Banking in a Free Society*, London, Institute of Economic Affairs.

Department of Environment (DOE) (1995), *Our Future Homes: Opportunity, Choice and Responsibility*, London, HMSO.

Department of Environment, Transport and the Regions (DETR) (2000), *Quality and Choice: A Decent Home for All*, London, DETR/DSS.

Department of Work and Pensions (DWP) (2002), *Building Choice and Responsibility: A Radical Agenda for Housing Benefit*, London, DWP.

Ferguson, N. (2008), *The Ascent of Money: A Financial History of the World*, London, Allen Lane.

Frey, B. and Stutzer, A. (eds) (2007), *Economics and Psychology: A Promising New Cross-disciplinary Field*, Cambridge, MA, MIT Press.

Garber, M. (2000), *Sex and Real Estate: Why We Love Houses*, New York, Anchor Books.

Gershon, M. (2007), *Heroic Conservatism: Why Republicans Need to Embrace America's Ideals (and Why They Deserve to Fail if They Don't)*, New York, Harper Collins.

Goff, S. (2009), 'House Price Movements Cause Confusion', *Financial Times*, 4/5 April, p. 3.

Greenspan, A. (2007), *The Age of Turbulence: Adventures in the New World*, London, Allen Lane.

Heilbrunn, J. (2008), *They Knew They Were Right: The Rise of the Neocons*, New York, Doubleday.

HM Treasury (2004), *Review of Housing Supply: Securing our Future Housing Needs*, London, HMSO (also known as the Barker Report).

Jacobs, K., Kemeny, J. and Manzi, T. (2003), 'Privileged or Exploited Council Tenants?: The Discursive Change in Conservative Housing Policy 1972–1980', *Policy and Politics*, 31, 3, pp. 307–20.

Jenkins, S. (1995), *Accountable to None: The Tory Nationalisation of Britain*, London, Hamish Hamilton.

Kemeny, J. (1981), *The Myth of Home Ownership: Public Versus Private Choices in Housing Tenure*, London, Routledge.

—— (2005), '"The Really Big Trade-off" Between Home Ownership and Welfare: Castles' Evaluation of the 1980 Thesis, and a Reformulation 25 Years on', *Housing Theory and Society*, 22, 2, pp. 59–75.

King, P. (1996), *The Limits of Housing Policy: A Philosophical Investigation*, London, Middlesex University Press.

—— (2000), 'Individuals and Competence', in King, P. and Oxley, M., *Housing: Who Decides?*, Basingstoke, Macmillan, pp. 9–69.

—— (2001), *Understanding Housing Finance*, London, Routledge.

—— (2003), *A Social Philosophy of Housing*, Aldershot, Ashgate.

—— (2004), *Private Dwelling: Contemplating the Use of Housing*, London, Routledge.

—— (2005), *The Common Place: The Ordinary Experience of Housing*, Aldershot, Ashgate.

—— (2006), *A Conservative Consensus?: Housing Policy Before 1997 and After*, Exeter, Imprint Academic.

—— (2008), *In Dwelling: Implacability, Exclusion and Acceptance*, Aldershot, Ashgate.

—— (2009), *Understanding Housing Finance: Meeting Needs and Making Choices*, 2nd edn, London, Routledge.

—— (2010), *Housing Policy Transformed: The Right to Buy and the Desire to Own*, Bristol, Policy Press.

Kristol, I. (1995), *Neo-conservatism: The Autobiography of an Idea: Selected Essays 1949–1995*, New York, Free Press.

Leunig, T. (2007), *In My Backyard: Unlocking the Planning System*, London, Centreforum.

Malpass, P. and Murie, A. (1999), *Housing Policy and Practice*, 5th edn, Basingstoke, Macmillan.

Mandeville, B. (1988), *The Fable of the Bees: Or Private Vices, Publick Benefits*, 2 vols, Indianapolis, IN, Liberty Classics.

Mill, J. S. [1859] (1974), *On Liberty*, London, Penguin.

Murray, C. (1984), *Losing Ground: American Social Policy 1950–1980*, New York, Basic Books.

Nozick, R. (1974), *Anarchy, State and Utopia*, Oxford, Blackwell.

Office of the Deputy Prime Minister (ODPM) (2003), *Sustainable Communities: Building for the Future*, London, ODPM.

——, *Sustainable Communities: Homes for All: A Five Year Plan from the ODPM*, London, ODPM.

Pickard, J. (2009), 'Brown Told to Put £6bn into Social Housing', *Financial Times*, 23 February, p. 2.

Pignal, S. (2008), 'Double Whammy Hampers Recovery', *Financial Times*, 19 December, p. 18.

Ronald, R. (2008), *The Ideology of Home Ownership: Homeownership Societies and the Role of Housing*, Basingstoke, Palgrave Macmillan.

Scholtes, S. (2009), 'Bargains Belie Lingering Housing Fears', *Financial Times*, 22 April, p. 8.

Shiller, R. (2005), *Irrational Exuberance*, 2nd edn, Princeton, NJ, Princeton University Press.

—— (2008), *The Sub-prime Solution: How Today's Global Financial Crisis Happened and What to do About It*, Princeton, NJ, Princeton University Press.

Smith, S. J. and Munro, M. (2008a), 'The Microstructures of Housing Markets', *Housing Studies*, 23, 2, pp. 159–62.

—— and —— (eds) (2008b), *The Microstructures of Housing Markets*, London, Routledge.

Sowell, T. (2007), *Basic Economics: A Common Sense Guide to the Economy*, 3rd edn, New York, Basic Books.

Stelzer, I. (ed.) (2004), *Neoconservatism*, London, Atlantic Books.

Thaler, R. and Sunstein, C. (2008), *Nudge: Improving Decisions about Health, Wealth, and Happiness*, New Haven, CT, Yale University Press.

Turner, G. (2008), *The Credit Crunch: Housing Bubbles, Globalisation and the World Economic Crisis*, London, Pluto.

Turner, J. (1976), *Housing by People: Towards Autonomy in Building Environments*, London, Marion Boyars.

Ubel, P. (2009), *Free Market Madness: Why Human Nature is at Odds with Economics – and Why It Matters*, Cambridge, MA, Harvard Business Press.

Ward, A. (2009), 'President to Help 9m Mortgage Holders', *Financial Times*, 19 February, p. 9.

Wilcox, S. (2008), *UK Housing Review, 2007/2008*, York, Chartered Institute of Housing/Council for Mortgage Lenders.

Williams, P. (1997), 'Introduction: Directions in Housing Policy', in Williams, P. (ed.), *Directions in Housing Policy: Towards Sustainable Housing Policies for the UK*, London, Paul Chapman, pp. 1–6.

Wolf, M. (2009), *Fixing Global Capitalism*, New Haven, CT, Yale University Press.

# Index

regularity 21–2, 48
Right to Buy 67, 68–9, 71, 90, 91,
   94, 142
risk sharing 118–9
Roosevelt F. D. 67

**S**

savings and loans 67
Shiller, R. 9, 39, 40, 46
social construction of owner
   occupation 8–9
social housing 94–6, 129
Sowell, T. 124
spending behaviour 37–9
Standard & Poor 78

sub-prime mortgages 70, 77–81,
   83, 86–77, 93–4, 142
subjective value 52–3, 60
Sustainable Communities Plan 117

**T**

Thatcher, M. 7, 68, 87, 109
Turner, J. 28–9, 55–7

**U**

unintended consequences 102

**W**

wholesale money markets 79, 80,
   81, 111

www.tandf.co.uk/journals/chos

# HOUSING STUDIES

Managing Editors:
**Chris Leishman** and **Moira Munro,** *University of Glasgow, UK,* and
**Charles E. Connerly,** (North American Editor), *University of Iowa, USA*
Editors: **Rowland Atkinson,** *University of York, UK* and
**Ray Forrest,** *City University of Hong Kong, Hong Kong*

### 2008 Impact Factor: 0.609
© 2009 Thomson Reuters, *2008 Journal Citation Reports®*

*Housing Studies* is the essential international forum for academic debate in the housing field. Since its establishment *Housing Studies* has become a leading housing journal and has played a major role in theoretical and analytical developments within this area of study.

*Housing Studies* is not limited in its geographical scope and welcomes contributions on housing and housing related issues in any national or crossnational context. The journal also provides an outlet for contributions from many different disciplines.

Recent articles include:

- **Dematerialising Money? Observations on the Flow of Wealth from Housing to Other Things**
  Susan J. Smith and Beverley A. Searle

- **Housing and the New Welfare State: Wobbly Pillar or Cornerstone?**
  Peter Malpass

- **Understanding Neighbourhood Housing Markets: Regional Context, Disequilibrium, Sub-markets and Supply**
  Glen Bramley, Chris Leishman and David Watkins

### View selected free articles at:
### www.tandf.co.uk/journals/chos

Routledge
Taylor & Francis Group

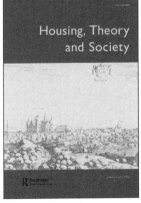